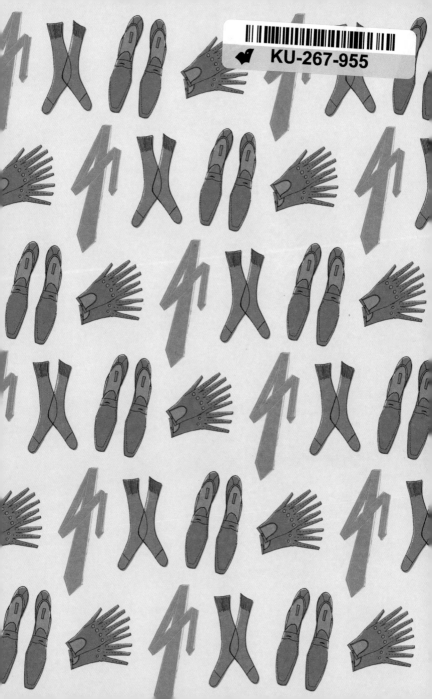

KU-267-955

The

Perfectly
Dressed
Gentleman

The Perfectly Dressed Gentleman

Robert O'Byrne

Illustrations by Lord Dunsby

CICO BOOKS

LONDON NEW YORK

Published in 2011 by CICO Books
An imprint of Ryland Peters & Small Ltd

20–21 Jockey's Fields   519 Broadway, 5th Floor
London WC1R 4BW   New York, NY 10012

www.cicobooks.com

10 9 8 7 6 5 4 3 2 1

Text © Robert O'Byrne 2011
Design and illustration © CICO Books 2011

The author's moral rights have been asserted. All rights reserved. No
part of this publication may be reproduced, stored in a retrieval system,
or transmitted in any form or by any means, electronic, mechanical,
photocopying, or otherwise, without the prior permission of the publisher.

A CIP catalog record for this book is
available from the Library of Congress
and the British Library.

ISBN: 978 1 907563 88 1

Printed in China

Editor: Pete Jorgensen

Designer: Paul Tilby

Illustrator: Lord Dunsby aka Steve Millington,
www.lorddunsby.co.uk

For digital editions visit
www.cicobooks.com/apps.php

contents

Introduction

As many definitions of what constitutes a gentleman exist as naysayers prepared to decry the decline in gentlemanly standards. "A true gentleman," said Oscar Wilde, "is one who is never unintentionally rude," while the 18th-century English physician Dr Thomas Fuller pronounced that a gentleman "is a man who can disagree without being disagreeable." However, universal agreement will never be reached on what attributes are necessary for someone to be esteemed a gentleman, not least because the term itself has long been in a state of evolution.

The word gentle derives from the Latin adjective *gentilis* meaning "of or belonging to the same family, group, or race." The notion of a gentleman emerged during the Middle Ages when such men, while not necessarily noble, were individuals entitled and expected to bear arms in defense of their monarch and country. In other words, they were members of a warrior caste.

This narrow definition of gentlemanliness began to broaden in the Renaissance with the emergence of princely courts at which the well-bred and wealthy were required to be in attendance. In order to flourish in the competitive courtly environment, men had to learn how to behave in company, a process assisted by the publication of guides to civility such as Baldassare Castiglione's *Il Libro del Cortegiano* (The Book of the Courtier), which appeared in 1528.

This stressed not only the importance of skill at arms but also the advantages of good manners, and how to be polite and considerate. Instruction from informed sources was of importance, but so too was moving in well-bred society: An English proverb has it that "Education begins a gentleman, conversation completes him."

Castiglione's book had enormous influence throughout Europe during the following centuries and helped to formulate the modern definition of a gentleman, one that gradually became dependent not so much on birth as behavior. This interpretation of gentlemanliness fully emerged in the 19th century with the rise of a bourgeoisie whose male members enjoyed the advantages of money but not high social rank. They wished to be regarded as gentlemen and so sought to emphasize the value of education and good manners.

While of primary significance today, this aspect of the gentleman's character has probably always been present to some extent. As the priest John Ball rhetorically asked during the Peasants' Revolt of 1381, "When Adam delved and Eve span, who then was the gentleman?" And in the 17th century a woman supposedly once asked James II to make her son a gentleman, to which the king responded, "I could make him a nobleman, but God Almighty could not make him a gentleman." In other words, regardless of origins anyone can be judged a gentleman provided he conforms to certain behavioral strictures, such as displaying consideration for other people. Different cultures will have their own rules of etiquette but a concern for the needs of society at large and an interest in the welfare of those he encounters are the hallmarks of the modern gentleman.

What does any of this have to do with clothing and how we men dress ourselves? More than you might appreciate. Once we move out of our private space and into the public arena, we should give thought to our appearance and whether it might cause disquiet or even offense. It could be, and often is, argued that how each of us dresses ought to be a matter of personal concern and irrelevant to anyone else. Whether it is piercings and tattoos or low-slung jeans that expose underwear, claims of personal expression are justified with the same defense: It's my business how I dress. In theory a case can be made on such grounds, but it presumes our own opinions and interests are more important than those of the rest of society. Because a gentleman would never agree with such an assertion, it follows that in matters of dress, as in every other aspect of his life, he will always give consideration to the interests of the world in which he moves, however irrational they might seem. If, for example, he receives a wedding invitation stipulating a formal dress code, this is what he will wear. To do otherwise would be to put his own inclinations ahead of his hosts' and that would be ungentlemanly. What some might castigate as conformism, a gentleman regards as consideration.

A gentleman takes both personal and public interest into account and dresses accordingly. That way he pleases not only himself but whoever meets him.

Points to Consider for Gentlemanly Dressing

✼ There should be nothing ostentatious about your appearance, nothing flash or attention-seeking. Elegant understatement is your hallmark: Observers will note that you are well dressed without necessarily being able to state precisely why.

✼ The value of cleanliness cannot be overstated. It does not matter how good are your clothes if the body beneath has not been thoroughly washed. Personal grooming is of the utmost importance and even supposedly minor details—the state of your nails, the line of hair on the back of your neck—must never be ignored. Every fine painting is composed of tiny individual details, all of which contribute to a successful whole. The same is true of your appearance: Overlook any one element of it and you risk impairing the finished result.

✼ Clothes should be kept in spotless condition, something not difficult to achieve provided you look after your wardrobe on a daily basis. Never wear the same item two days in succession, hang up or fold away garments after they have been worn, attend to stains and marks as soon as possible. Think reciprocity: The better you look after your clothes, the better they will make you look. In addition, taking care of your clothes means they will last longer and therefore amply repay the expense of their purchase. Not looking after your wardrobe is a waste of money.

✼ Know yourself. Become familiar with your body, and what you can and cannot wear. Your height, shape, and coloring ought to play a part in decisions about dress. As will be pointed out in the coming chapters, certain items of clothing flatter tall more than short men, slim more than stout. A man who understands his physique is more likely to be reckoned well dressed than someone with no awareness of himself.

✻ Buy the best you can afford. This is especially important as regards footwear since bad shoes can damage your feet. Price should not be confused with quality: Just because an item is expensive does not mean it is good. Therefore learn how to inspect any garment before you make a purchase, reading the fabric composition and care instructions, and turning the piece inside out to check the caliber of stitching.

✻ Always think through your entire outfit with the intention of producing a harmonious whole. While everything you wear does not have to match precisely—indeed it will be the better for not doing so—each item should complement the rest, and no one article of clothing should overwhelm everything else.

✻ Don't equate conformity with conservatism. While the rules of gentlemanly dress should not be broken, they will prove flexible. Your clothes ought to provide an indication of your personality even while they are consistent with the accepted norms of dress. Within the strictest codes there remains room for interpretation.

✻ Enjoy yourself. Choosing your clothes and dressing well should enhance your day, not encumber it. Learn to take pleasure in your appearance and you are more likely to give pleasure to others. By so doing, you will prove yourself a perfect—and perfectly dressed—gentleman.

Chapter 1

The Suit

**Contrary to popular opinion, a good suit can serve
an infinite variety of roles and be adapted to almost
any circumstance. Just as many women rely on an
LBD (Little Black Dress) to see them through many
different occasions, so a gentleman will find a Good
Dark Suit—which should perhaps henceforth be
known as the GDS—invaluable.**

———◆———

The Origins of the Suit

In the pages ahead, it will be stated more than once that men's
clothing as it exists today originated in England at the start of the
19th century and is particularly indebted to one man: George "Beau"
Brummell. But the suit's starting point goes back further, to the 17th
century and the restoration of Charles II to the English throne. Prior
to this period, the suit did not exist; while men may have worn short
jackets, they were teamed with doublet and hose.

In February 1661 diarist Samuel Pepys noted that he had worn his
"coate," which was "the manner now among gentlemen." The coate
in question was of a length similar to the modern overcoat and was a
somewhat fitted variation on a garment worn by men when riding.
Five years later, in October 1666 Pepys recorded that the king "begins

to put on his vest," this being what Americans still know as a vest but the British call a waistcoat. Thus the three-piece suit began to appear, especially when English countrymen who, unlike their French counterparts, did not care to attend court had such sets of clothing made in the same plain wool cloth to wear at home on their country estates.

Anglomania in respect of clothing has a long history and one of its key dates is the publication in 1774 of the German writer Johann Wolfgang von Goethe's *The Sorrows of Young Werther*. The hero of this proto-romantic novel dresses in the English style—that is to say in a plain tailcoat, vest/waistcoat, trousers, and boots—and Goethe's book inspired a mania among sensitive young men to dress likewise. One of the features of the French Revolution was the emergence of the Sans-culottes—the men whose break with the Ancien Régime was symbolized by their abandonment of court knee breeches in preference for English-style suiting.

Brummell paid particular attention to the perfection of silhouette, achieved through careful cut of fabric and exact tailoring

In the opening years of the 19th century, the most significant contribution made by Beau Brummell was to work with tailors in London. Together they focused on creating clothes that fitted the body and followed its line precisely; prior to Brummell's appearance this had not been deemed a matter of importance. Brummell was a plain dresser, unconcerned with rich fabrics or elaborate finishes. Instead he concentrated on perfection of silhouette, achieved through careful cut of fabric and exact tailoring. His rise in influence coincided with an increasing sophistication among London's tailors, many of whom, then as now, were based in Savile Row, Mayfair. The simple but supremely elegant style of dress advocated by both Brummell and his tailors was soon universally adopted, hence the emergence of the Good Dark Suit that remains an indispensable feature of the male wardrobe.

The Suit Today

Although once almost revolutionary in its connotations, for the past half-century the suit has come to be associated with conservatism and is shunned by any aspiring radical. On the other hand, all men who wish to be considered respectable and conforming members of society will don a suit. For similar reasons, some men own what they designate their "interview suit," a somber item worn whenever they wish to make a good impression. Suits are also associated with formal occasions, not just a job interview but also weddings, funerals, and so forth. They can be judged stuffy and uncomfortable, although anyone who finds them so is clearly not wearing a well-designed piece of clothing because a good suit should be as imperceptible to the wearer as a second skin.

You will find a good suit enhances your wardrobe and its absence will leave you sartorially poorer

In the 1990s some businesses that had hitherto expected their employees to wear a suit abandoned this prerequisite, and many newer companies, especially those in the technology sector, began almost to frown on suits as somehow inhibiting creativity. Nevertheless, certain professions like banking and law, as well as senior management in most fields, still expect their practitioners to wear a suit, as do large sections of the service industry. Thus the derogatory term "suits" describes men who are believed to have sacrificed their individuality to corporate conventionality. This is a mistaken view: You will find the possession of a good suit enhances your wardrobe and its absence will leave you sartorially poorer than should be the case. No man who aspires to be well dressed can do without a suit.

Bespoke

The term bespoke, which means custom-made, derives from having a cloth or garment "spoken for." In other words, it is the male equivalent of women's couture: something made specifically to your measurements by an accredited tailor. Ideally you should own at least one bespoke suit. It goes without saying that acquiring such an item is going to be an expensive enterprise but this will prove a worthwhile investment.

A bespoke suit is as good as a gym membership—both make sure you take care of yourself

Whereas most women are familiar with their body size and shape, the same is not true of the average male. Next time you're in a public place, look at the men around you and notice how if they are wearing a jacket, almost without exception this is the wrong size; most commonly it will be too big for the frame beneath. A tailor will provide you with correct measurements, those specific to your body (most men's shoulders, for example, slope more on one side than the other), a piece of information that will be invaluable when you subsequently buy ready-to-wear clothing. In addition, the high cost of purchasing a bespoke suit ensures that you take care of both the garment and your body—there's no point in spending all that money and then six months later discovering that you've put on weight and can no longer fit into the pants or button the jacket. In this respect, a bespoke suit is as good as a gym membership—both make sure you take care of yourself.

Creating the Perfect Fit

The process of having a bespoke suit made for you is as follows. You begin by consulting your chosen tailor over such matters as cut, cloth, and style of the garment before careful measurements of your body are taken. A pattern is then made specific to you, and this will be used to chalk out and cut the selected fabric. After lining, canvases, pockets, buttons, and so forth have been also prepared, the individual parts are sewn together in anticipation of a first fitting on the client. This is called the baste stage, after which a new pattern may have to be created, the suit stitching ripped out, the cloth recut, and other necessary adjustments made. Additional structural work is now performed before a second fitting. At this stage, the suit ought to fit the client without fault, but, should it be required, further alterations will be made before collar and sleeves are sewn in, buttonholes and edge stitching completed by hand, and so on. Then, after a final press, the finished garment is ready for a last fitting and presentation.

 It will be appreciated that length of time and attention to detail account for the cost of a bespoke suit. As a less expensive alternative, there is made-to-measure in which many of the same processes are followed, but rather than a new pattern being made, an existing one that most closely corresponds to the client's measurements is used, albeit with individual adjustments. In addition, whereas bespoke involves hand-sewing, made-to-measure uses machine stitching, although some details may be finished by hand. Obviously price is a factor here, with made-to-measure being notably cheaper but still providing a better fit than does ready-to-wear, which depends on average sizing and fails to take the particular customer's body shape into account.

The Business Suit

The most common suit style worn today is the business suit, also known as the lounge suit in Britain. As already mentioned, the suit evolved from clothing worn by country gentlemen and, despite its name, this is also true of the business suit. There are enormous variations within the basic theme, depending on whether the suit in question closes with one, two, or three buttons, is single- or double-breasted, has a single or double vent at the back, and so forth. Then there are decisions to be made about the cloth, cut, color, and pattern.

When these factors are taken into account, it becomes evident that the reason for the suit's enduring success is its versatility: No two need ever be the same. It is no wonder that in recent decades so many women, appreciating its innumerable merits, have also adopted the suit as their preferred mode of dress.

The Jacket

The key element in the suit is the jacket, since this determines the overall silhouette. It is also the part of any suit over which most trouble will have been taken in production.

Button Placement

Jackets are either single- or double-breasted. Shorter and heavier-built men are advised to keep away from the double-breasted style since it will only draw attention to their physique. Only half the outside buttons on a double-breasted jacket function because the second row is solely for show. There are typically four or six buttons in total, with the upper pair being half again as far apart as each of the lower pairs. A double-breasted jacket can look extremely stylish provided it is well tapered from shoulder to waist. Otherwise, as was the fashion in the 1980s, it will seem excessively boxy.

> *Always leave the bottom button of your jacket unfastened, not least because this will make it easier for you to put a hand in your pants pocket*

The male jacket buttons left side over right, supposedly because in the days when swords were carried a right-handed man could reach for the hilt of his weapon with ease. If you are portly, wear a single-breasted jacket with lower placed buttons as this will increase the vertical line and make you look leaner. Jackets usually have either two or three buttons but you will also find examples with a single-button fastening; these are usually darted to give a narrow outline and therefore look best on slim men. If closing the front of your jacket, only use the upper button (with a two-button fastening) or the middle one (with three). If you insist on buttoning through your jacket, it will have the effect of making you appear constrained. Always leave the bottom button unfastened, not least because this will make it easier for you to put a hand into your pants pocket. Likewise, when you sit down unbutton your jacket, otherwise it will strain against your body (and you also risk creasing it across the back). Your jacket ought to fasten comfortably over the chest and not gape open when buttoned; if it does so, then you're wearing too large a size.

The Correct Fit

In addition a jacket should fit tidily across the back and not hang off the shoulders; the last of these is a common failing precisely because men are unfamiliar with their correct size. Because of the English tradition in tailoring, English suits tend to have defined but not exaggerated shoulder lines, a tapered side, and two vents at the back, all contributing to a Y-shaped silhouette. Italian suits, which became fashionable in the 1980s, have a stronger, wider shoulder line—even when, as introduced by Giorgio Armani, they have no padding— and hang looser on the torso without vents at the back. American suits occupy a ground somewhere between these two, with a certain amount of both shoulder definition and tapering.

Lapel Styles

The jacket lapel derives from 18th-century coats which buttoned up to the neck. When the top of the coat was left open, the ends of the closure fell back to expose the lining, and during the following century this feature of the jacket was gradually formalized into the creased lapels we know, fronted in the same fabric as the rest of the garment with the lining no longer visible.

There are different styles of lapels: the notched or stepped which only befits single-breasted suits, the peaked (much seen on double-breasted suits and dinner jackets), the shawl, and others such as Mandarin collars. On a single-breasted, sharply tapered suit a peaked lapel can look extremely smart. The left lapel should have a buttonhole intended to hold a boutonniere, which is a decorative flower.

The Purpose of Pockets

Jackets tend to have a variety of interior and exterior pockets. Those inside the jacket are intended to hold items such as wallets and in recent years cell phones, but it is advisable not to put too much into them as it distorts the garment's shape. On the outside, there will be one upper breast pocket on the left-hand side; this can hold a pocket handkerchief either decorative or functional in intent. Below will be two pockets, one each at left and right. The patch pocket is a single piece of cloth stitched onto the jacket; essentially casual in style, it suits sports and linen jackets but does not become formal suiting. The flap pocket is seen on most business suits, the pocket being contained inside the main body of the jacket and marked by a lined flap of fabric. These pockets run in a horizontal line except in instances where the pocket is slanted (called a hacking pocket because it was first created to allow a hand to slip easily into the pocket while out riding). On the right-hand side of the jacket you sometimes find another, smaller pocket above the main flap pocket; this is known as a ticket pocket, its original purpose being to hold a train ticket.

Finally, formalwear such as the dinner jacket usually has two jetted pockets, enclosed within the garment with the slit marked by a small strip of fabric along the top. Jackets usually come with their pockets stitched shut; it is advisable to leave them this way to stop you using the pockets to carry items and ruining the line of your garment.

Sleeve Length

Jacket sleeves should not be baggy but nor ought they to be cut so tight that it becomes impossible to lift your arms over your head with ease. Jacket sleeves end in a row of buttons which traditionally could be undone; where this is still possible the style has the self-explanatory name of "surgeon's cuff." Rarely found in ready-to-wear, these remain a distinguishing feature of bespoke suits. Otherwise cuff buttons are purely decorative and number anywhere between one and four, the latter being most common today on business suit jackets. The ideal jacket cuff length should allow about half an inch (1cm) of the shirt beneath to be seen. A century ago, some jacket sleeves had turn-back cuffs two inches (5cm) deep and these are still occasionally seen.

The ideal jacket cuff length should allow about half an inch of the shirt beneath to be seen

One Vent or Two?

The vent on the tail of your jacket once served the purpose of allowing the wearer to ride a horse without sitting on his coat. While this may no longer be the case, they still help to ensure the hang of a jacket is preserved, especially while sitting down. Italian-designed and some casual jackets tend to have no vent, but the alternatives are a single or double vent, the second of these being typical of English tailoring. As a rule, dinner jackets do not have vents.

Fabric

One of the great, but rarely acknowledged, changes in clothing to have occurred over the past century is the weight of our clothes; today, thanks to better heating at home and in the workplace, we dress more lightly than did our forebears. As a consequence of central heating all sorts of new fabric blends have been created, especially by Italian mills, to offer the consumer more flexibility and ease of dressing.

Nevertheless, when it comes to suiting, nothing is better than medium-weight worsted pure wool, preferably taken from merino sheep. Despite recent competition from new fibers, wool remains the best choice for a gentleman's suit because it is natural, breathes well, provides good insulation, and is exceptionally durable (thanks to their natural elasticity, wool fibers resist tearing and can bend back on themselves more than 20,000 times without breaking, unlike cotton which breaks after 3,200 bends). Made from wool, worsted yarns are hard-wearing and yet light, and therefore much used for suiting. During the course of the last century, they were produced in ever-finer weights and are now the cloth of choice for city suits.

Wool Variants

Tweed is a woolen fabric with an altogether rougher finish, suitable for countrywear being moisture-resistant and hard-wearing. The two most famous tweeds are Harris from Scotland and Donegal from Ireland, but lighter, finer tweeds, some of them incorporating varying quantities of silk, are also produced elsewhere. Tweed remains an essentially rural cloth and as a rule is not seen in an urban setting, except when used for a weekend jacket.

Invented in 1879 by Thomas Burberry (founder of the still extant clothing company), gabardine is another tough, tightly woven woolen cloth appropriate for suiting and identifiable by its diagonal ribbed surface.

Mohair is a silk-like cloth with a characteristic high sheen that comes from the Angora goat. Warm, water-resistant, and durable, it is considered a luxury fiber, as is cashmere which likewise comes from goats and is particularly fine and smooth to the touch.

Flannel is a soft woven fabric made from carded wool. It used to be popular for business suiting—in the mid-1950s author Sloan Wilson wrote a best-selling novel called *The Man in the Gray Flannel Suit*—but has since fallen out of favor and now tends to be more often used for casual jackets.

Alternative Fabrics

Jackets and suits are sometimes made of velvet and its near relation corduroy, with the former fabric most often employed in the production of evening wear. The best, and most expensive, velvet is made of silk, with a less costly version produced in cotton. In recent years technological advances have led to the creation of a variety of entirely synthetic velvets, or velvets produced from a mix of natural and man-made fibers. The tufted pile of velvet gives it a uniquely tactile quality, enhanced by the cloth's reflective sheen, hence the appeal for evening wear.

Corduroy is in effect a ridged variant of velvet, with alternating tufts and patches of bare base fabric. Corduroy can have different widths, the size of which is known as the "wale," this being the number of ridges per inch (2.5cm), so the lower the wale, the thicker the raised tufts. Standard wale of 11 per inch is used for pants, while jackets are most often made of pincord or needlecord corduroy with a wale of 16 or more per inch.

A number of lighter-weight cloths are used for summer suiting and, while these will not necessarily find a place in the office environment, they are ideal for occasions when semiformal dressing is required. Among the most notable fabrics is cotton, in particular when manufactured as seersucker. First used for suits in colonial India, seersucker is so woven that some threads bunch together to give the finished cloth an uneven surface, which in turn means it sits slightly away from the surface of the skin and is cool to wear. Seersucker often comes in stripes of white and another color, commonly blue or gray.

Linen has long been used for summer suiting. The textile is made from fibers of the flax plant and is renowned for its absorbent qualities and coolness. With a natural luster, it can be dyed almost any color, but for suit jackets and pants is commonly white or ivory. Linen absorbs and loses moisture with ease, but it soon becomes wrinkled and for some men this is a drawback because their appearance can thus look crumpled. On the other hand, that slightly battered quality is part of its charm and linen grows softer with age and washing, making it also popular for casual shirts. Whether you take to it rather depends on how sharply turned out you wish to be on all occasions.

Color and Pattern

If you're going to own only one top-notch suit, best make it in a single color and one that offers maximum versatility. Black is funereal and oppressive (and, you'll soon discover, shows every speck of dirt). Blue is an option but finding the right shade of navy—not too dark but not too bright either—can take up a lot of time. Frankly, brown for city suits is simply not to be countenanced; it is essentially a country color and looks out of place in the urban environment. Charcoal gray, on the other hand, complements every skin tone, works with every color and pattern of shirt, and successfully manages the dressed-up/dressed-down formula. A good medium-weight gray suit is at home in the business environment, plus the jacket can be worn without the pants and instead teamed with jeans or chinos. So, a charcoal gray suit should be the centerpiece of your classic wardrobe. Of course you really should have more than a single suit, particularly if you are obliged to wear one every day. No garment can be worn on successive days without suffering; it should be left to rest in between. If you buy judiciously, wait for seasonal sales to make your purchases. Stick to classic styles and take trouble to look after your clothes and it should be possible very quickly to build up a collection of good suits that will last you for many years to come.

Charcoal gray complements all skin tones, works with every color and pattern of shirt, and capably manages the dressed-up or dressed-down formula

Acceptable Patterns

With a few extreme exceptions, suit patterns are limited to herringbone, stripes, and checks, but do not be discouraged by this apparent restriction. Rather like suit styling, within a supposedly tight framework the imaginative dresser will discover the possibilities of almost infinite variety.

Herringbone is created by cloth being made in a broken-twill weave. This produces threads running alternately from left to right and forming an inverted V-effect not unlike the bones of a herring. Usually in wool, it is very popular for suiting.

Stripes traditionally take two forms: the chalk and the pin, with the first being visibly wider than the second. They can be found on cloth of all colors, usually black, blue, and gray. The vertical stripe is especially advantageous for shorter or stockier men, since it gives the impression of lengthening their silhouette. Pinstripe has become associated with two very different sectors of society: banking and the Mafia, both of which want to convey respectability, albeit for dissimilar reasons. Although it can sometimes look stuffy, when seen on a well-cut suit pinstripe or chalk-stripe is immensely stylish.

Pinstripe has become associated with two very different sectors of society: banking and the Mafia

More variation is found in suit checks, among the more popular being houndstooth, a duotone pattern achieved by intertwining dark and light threads to produce a small checkered effect supposedly resembling the teeth of a dog. The other common check is glen plaid, a woven twill design intermingling small and large checks, usually in black and white but perhaps incorporating a third color. Glen plaid is also known as Prince of Wales check, since it was often worn by the Duke of Windsor while he held the former title. Glen plaid can be smart but, as with so much else, should be worn with care by the heavily built. Incidentally, tartan must be avoided by anyone who is not Scottish or a punk.

Other Styles of Jackets

In addition to suits, your wardrobe should hold a number of other jackets which will come into their own on semiformal and casual occasions. Here are the main categories.

The tweed jacket is a hardy perennial, not least thanks to the varieties of weights, colors, and patterns in which tweed is available. Such jackets started to be worn in the middle of the 19th century, initially by ghillies (fishing/hunting guides) and gamekeepers on Scottish estates but their practical appeal meant similar items were soon being produced for the owners of these estates and their friends, and demand quickly spread ever wider until today when the tweed jacket enjoys universal appeal. With its lightly defined shoulder line, single or double vent, and front flap pockets, you will find ownership of one or more tweed jackets invaluable, since they are highly adaptable, working well with any style of pants, shirt, or knitwear, capable of being smartened up or toned down according to what is worn with them. Choose tweed of medium weight as you do not want to become overly hot while wearing the jacket.

The hacking jacket is most often made of tweed but has a couple of particular characteristics, not least the diagonally slanting pockets which indicate the jacket's origins as a style to be worn when on horseback (the pocket being so shaped that they were easier for the rider to access in these circumstances). Hacking jackets as a rule have strongly defined shoulders, a darted body to define the waist, a high-buttoning front, and a single rear vent. They may be made of tweed or some other hard-wearing cloth, such as cavalry twill or gabardine.

The sports jacket is another variation on the same theme, often made in cashmere (or a wool/cashmere mix), flannel, or something similar. It will usually have patch pockets and be relaxed in styling with a loose cut to the body.

The blazer takes its name from the bright red cloth used to make the jackets first worn by the rowing club of St John's College, Cambridge in 1825; another legend has it that the term derives from the jackets worn by sailors on *HMS Blazer* but this is frequently called into question. In fact, the garment worn by the Cambridge rowers was closer to what would now be called a boating jacket than the blazer, which stylistically is a descendant of the reefer jacket, also known as the pea coat, a double-breasted garment worn by sailors when they were engaged in activities such as reefing a ship's sails. These jackets gradually evolved into the modern blazer and became single- as well as double-breasted, and made of lightweight wool. This variation is only one of many that can be found in blazers today, since they might have flap or patch pockets and horn or metal buttons (a memory of their naval origins), and be cut close to the body or have a more relaxed shape.

But whatever its attributes, every blazer will be navy in color and possess the same quality as a good tweed jacket: the ability to be called into service in almost every circumstance. You can wear a blazer with a shirt and tie or with an open-necked polo shirt. It can be accompanied with equal success by gray flannel pants, jeans, or even shorts. In other words, it is highly adaptable and for that reason you owe it to yourself to have one. Blazers, habitually with a badge on the breast pocket or some colored piping around lapels and cuffs, are worn to indicate membership of a club or sporting organization, or else attendance at a particular school or college.

The Waistcoat

The origins of the waistcoat, or the vest as it is also known, can be precisely dated. In October 1666, Samuel Pepys wrote in his diary that Charles II "hath yesterday in council declared his resolution of setting a fashion for clothes which he will never alter. It will be a vest, I know not well how." This garment, today known as a waistcoat, was inspired by the vests seen by English travelers to the Persian court of Shah Abbas who brought news of them back to England.

For a long time, men's "vests" were as elaborate and richly embroidered as the coats worn over them. It was only when male dress underwent a radical purification in the early 19th century that waistcoats became less elaborate, although a residue of that old style can still be seen in the fancy waistcoats worn by men participating in formal occasions such as weddings. In addition, whereas the 17th- and 18th-century vests had been long, the modern waistcoat as it emerged in the Regency era was shorter, stopping at the waist (hence the term waistcoat). Dandies like Beau Brummell recognized the waistcoat's potential to enhance the rest of a man's costume, and to act as a figure-molder by exaggerating the chest (sometimes with the assistance of concealed padding) and pulling in the waist. With whalebone stiffeners at the front and lacings to the rear, Victorian waistcoats acted as surrogate corsets for men. Although these features later disappeared, the waistcoat remained a part of men's clothing until the mid-20th century, especially when a suit was being worn and in part because it provided additional warmth in cold weather.

Improvements in heating and the growth in popularity of knitwear led to a decline in waistcoat wearing, but there have been periodic revivals in popularity, such as when they were worn by John Travolta in 1977's *Saturday Night Fever*. And they have remained an essential part of dress among senior figures in certain professions like banking and law. Of course, many young men today wear waistcoats without an accompanying jacket and even without shirts, replacing the latter with a T-shirt.

Wearing Your Waistcoat

A classic waistcoat is made of the same fabric as the suit jacket and pants, will have six buttons and four pockets: two at the breast, two closer to the waistband. An adjustable strap at the back will help to tighten the lower section of the garment, the back being made either of the same material as the front or else of satin. It is traditional to leave the bottom button of the waistcoat unfastened, supposedly because this is what Edward VII did when his stomach had expanded in middle age. The waistcoat should end just below the waistband of your pants, so that no sign of the belt can be seen; a gap between the two is unsightly. Similarly, when the front of your jacket is fastened, only the topmost button of the waistcoat should be visible.

Whether a waistcoat has lapels or not is a matter of personal taste, but bear in mind that it will add extra fabric and therefore may bulk out the silhouette. Your waistcoat must sit flush with your chest and not bulge out, so it is important that the fit be correct. Tailors will confirm that this is a technically difficult garment to produce and it is easy for it to destroy rather than improve your overall appearance.

Suit Pants

Whether a waistcoat is present or not, no suit can be given such a name unless it features a matching jacket and pants. The second of these garments is usually given less attention than jackets are. But pants have to suffer the greater wear and tear, so if possible, buy two pairs when purchasing a new suit (especially if it is bespoke). Your pants should fit well around the waist and not need to be held up by a belt, even though you will, of course, wear one of these or else a pair of suspenders, known as braces in Britain. Pants that are too loose will leave puckered fabric around the waist and ruin the chances of producing a smooth line. Likewise the legs of your pants should be neither too tight nor too baggy, allowing easy movement when required.

Creases, Cuffs, and Pleats

The crease down the front of each leg is a relative innovation, dating only from the end of the 19th century, around the same time that cuffs, or turn-ups, at the bottom of pants also made their debut. Today a sharp-centered crease in your pants will always look smart, just as its absence will suggest scruffiness. The only pants in which center creases are not deemed acceptable are jeans; there is no logic in this opinion but it is widespread.

Cuffs are conventionally regarded as unsuitable for business suits and formal wear, but fine for more casual dressing. They ought to be between an inch and an inch and a half (2.5–4cm) in depth. Shorter men are advised not to adopt cuffs as they can have the effect of making a pant leg look shorter than is the case. With or without a cuff, pant legs ought to be long enough to "break" on the front of the shoe and then have a small single fold before they begin their rise.

Pleats at the front of pants were commonly seen in the 1980s and '90s but in recent years have been less popular. There may be anything between one and four pleats on pants; those opening toward the side pockets are called reverse pleats while those opening toward the center are called forward pleats. Flat-fronted pants convey a smoother overall look to a suit and also increase the impression of leg length. For a long time pant flies were fastened by buttons, a feature still found both on clothes produced by traditional companies and, by contrast, on jeans. On the other hand, zippers are easier to fasten and give the front of pants a flatter line.

Chapter 2

The Coat

Overcoats are extremely practical items of clothing and you ought to have several in your wardrobe, distinguished from one another by color and material which will, in turn, mark them out for different occasions. Today the primary function of an overcoat remains what it has always been: to exclude cold and dirt. Before the advent of central heating, the possession of a thick coat was more necessary than is now the case. Nevertheless, since all of us have to venture outdoors—even if only occasionally—they retain their purpose, especially as global warming seems to have made our winters colder than ever before.

***

Moreover, as is often remarked today, when a man sheds or dons his coat he also makes a statement, thereby either announcing his arrival or declaring his imminent departure. Likewise, retaining your coat while indoors announces more clearly than could any words an intention not to linger. Thus coats possess their own language, one further emphasized by variations in fabric weight, design, and shade.

A Coat to Suit the Occasion

Ideally you ought to own a decent winter coat of substance, one that will provide ample protection from the elements in cold weather. A second coat of lighter weight and intended for town wear is also advantageous. In addition you will want to possess a raincoat and perhaps a coat for evenings and formal occasions.

The last of these will be black, but the color of your other coats should depend on personal taste and the circumstances in which they are most often to be worn. If you live in the country, for example, a tweed coat in mixed colors might be suitable, while for city dwellers something in a wool/cashmere mix and a shade of dark blue or gray would be the best option. Other factors will determine length, longer coats hanging more kindly on the frames of tall, slim men than on those of their shorter, stouter counterparts. Likewise, double-breasted coats—which used to be the norm until the late Victorian era—rarely look well on men carrying extra weight, since they draw attention to this disposition; if you have a heavy build, opt for a single-breasted coat and never one with a belt, or it could focus the eye on your midriff.

Finally, an overcoat, when teamed with gloves, scarf, and perhaps a hat, "finishes" an ensemble and indicates to observers what it means to be properly dressed. Especially on formal occasions, a man without a coat will always look wanting.

Like so much of men's dress, the overcoat as we know it today is a descendant of early 19th-century fashion. As is often the case, coats owe at least some of their present characteristics to military dress— the length of the coat and its vent at the back cut high meaning this garment could be worn while riding a horse, and still keep the wearer well covered and warm.

Choosing a Style

Some styles of coats are little seen today, such as the Ulster, which was made of a hard-wearing fabric like tweed and came with a shoulder cape over the sleeves; this feature disappeared around the beginning of the 20th century and the Ulster has been in decline ever since. So too the Inverness, a formal coat with long winged open sleeves that used to be worn with evening dress.

On the other hand, the Chesterfield, which originated in the 19th century, is the ancestor of most of today's overcoats. It is long, to the

knees or even a little below, with no horizontal seam around the waist or sidebodies and a plain back, but the body can be somewhat shaped by judicious use of side seams and darts. A staple of the modern man's wardrobe, the Chesterfield can be either single- or double-breasted and be made in various weights of wool, cashmere, or a mix of both. As a formal coat, its palette is limited to black, gray, and navy. The best-known manufacturer of the Chesterfield-style coat is Crombie, a Scottish company in business since 1805, the name of which has become generic for coats of this type.

The Chesterfield is the ancestor of most of today's coats and is a staple of the modern man's wardrobe

A variation on this theme is the covert coat, made in beige- or fawn-colored twill. Originally intended for the country, its relatively light weight means this item is now more often worn as a city coat with a suit beneath. The classic covert has a fly front closure, two side pockets (and a smaller ticket pocket), a velvet collar, and four lines of stitching at the cuffs and around the bottom hem.

The polo coat is an American variant of the Chesterfield, believed to date from a century ago when polo players sought something to throw over their shoulders for warmth between chukkers. It is immediately identifiable by being made from plush, honey-toned camel hair and double-breasted. Other features can include thick sleeve cuffs, patch pockets, a half- or full belt, and white mother-of-pearl buttons. There is something inherently luxurious about a polo coat and it has long been favored by the exceptionally wealthy, not least because it is a visibly expensive purchase.

The Raglan is not too dissimilar from the Chesterfield except that it lacks shoulder seams so that each sleeve's upper side runs straight to the neckline, with a diagonal seam from underarm to collarbone.

Its name comes from the 1st Baron Raglan, who lost his right arm following injuries that he sustained in 1815 at the Battle of Waterloo. The Raglan coat is customarily buttoned through, with a loose body and no belt.

Occasionally adopted by members of indie bands, the Duffel looks likely to remain a minority taste

The Loden coat is identifiable by its color, a deep green, and by its cloth, first woven by peasants living in the Austrian region of Loderers in the 16th century. The fabric is made from coarse oily wool of mountain sheep, which undergoes a process of shrinking so that it has the dense texture of felt before the nap is brushed and clipped, the result being a lightweight but tough cloth. Designed to be worn by huntsmen, the traditional Loden coat is unlined and has a deep center vent down the back (to allow freedom of movement), a double layer of material on the shoulders, and a covered fly-front.

Today the Duffel coat is liable to be associated with geeks, members of the old British Labour Party, and Paddington Bear; it is rarely the choice for anyone fashion-conscious. The name derives from the town of Duffel in Belgium where this style is believed to have originated. Aside from the coarse, heavy wool and tartan lining used in its production, the two other distinctive traits of the Duffel are its hood and its toggle fastenings. The coat is not darted, falling straight to just above the knee. Occasionally adopted by members of indie bands, the Duffel looks likely to remain a minority taste.

As already observed, in addition to these coats, you will want to own at least one garment suitable for giving protection from rain. The classic of this genre is the Mackintosh, named after its Scottish originator Charles Macintosh who began selling his patented waterproof coats of rubberized fabric in the mid-1820s. Traditional Mackintoshes, otherwise known as "macs," continue to be produced and sold today, both their method of manufacture and their design having been updated in the intervening two centuries. Nevertheless, an authentic coat must be made of rubberized or rubber-laminated fabric.

The Mackintosh should be distinguished from the trench coat, which as its name indicates was originally created to be worn by soldiers fighting in the trenches during World War I. They needed an alternative to their heavy wool greatcoats and a trench coat fitted the bill.

Two British companies, Aquascutum and Burberry, both lay claim to have invented this garment, but the latter certainly patented the cloth from which it was made: gabardine. Water- and wind-resistant, gabardine is a tough, tightly woven worsted wool or cotton twill weave. In style, the trench coat still shows its military origins, with shoulder tabs and cuff straps, a storm flap by the collar, and a belt carrying several D-shaped rings, the last of these allowing soldiers to attach various items of equipment to their coat. Unlike Mackintoshes, trench coats are not waterproof: Nor do they provide ample warmth in very cold weather. But in the aftermath of World War I they became popular among civilians and started to make regular appearances in films, often worn by private detectives and by anti-heroes such as Humphrey Bogart's Rick Blaine in 1942's *Casablanca*. The trench coat has never since lost its romantic aura.

In style, the trench coat still shows its military origins, with shoulder tabs and cuff straps, a storm flap by the collar, and a belt carrying several D-shaped rings

Finally, there is an item of clothing traditionally worn in the countryside but now as often seen in an urban setting: the Barbour. This is a coat made by J. Barbour & Sons Ltd, a British business established at the end of the 19th century and renowned for the hardy construction and durability of its waterproof waxed cotton fabric. Among aficionados, at least part of a Barbour's appeal is precisely its apparent indestructibility; the older and more battered the coat, the more it is cherished. Although the company has created new designs to take into account contemporary taste, the original Barbour cannot really be described as an object of great beauty. On the other hand, whatever the style it will keep the wearer warm and dry, and this helps to explain why city dwellers have adopted the Barbour in such large numbers.

Chapter 3

Shirts

The world's oldest preserved garment, dating back to around 3000 BCE. and made of linen, is a shirt discovered in Egypt by the archaeologist Flinders Petrie in 1912. This demonstrates that despite undergoing various permutations over the centuries, the shirt has been a staple of men's dressing for at least five millennia.

Originally it was a tunic, often worn loose and made of linen; both characteristics demonstrated the wearer's wealth because only the affluent could afford the extravagance of such an ample garment made in this costly fabric. In the 16th century, the shirt as we now know it began to emerge, albeit heavily ornamented with lace and other fripperies at the wrist and around the neck. These were dispensed with in the post-French Revolution era, when simplicity of style began to be prized: Remember the Regency dandy Beau Brummell's axiom, "No perfumes but fine linen, plenty of it, and country washing."

The present form of plain, buttoned, and closely fitted cotton shirt only achieved widespread popularity in the 19th century as the urban middle class grew in number and needed to develop a practical wardrobe. The shirt with fastening cuffs and collar answered this requirement, although from around 1820 the collar was detachable, allowing it to be changed more frequently than the main part of the garment; this was because the collar most obviously showed dirt and signs of wear. In addition, it could be starched to retain stiffness while the rest of the shirt was left soft. The attached collar gradually grew in popularity in the first decades of the 20th century and is now the norm. But whatever its shape and fabric, a good shirt remains every gentleman's best friend; even today, to lose the shirt off one's back remains the ultimate symbol of shame.

Achieving the Perfect Shape

If you are not familiar with the manufacturer, it is always worth trying on a shirt before purchase, since there is now such a variety of construction methods that not all garments hang on the torso in the same way. You should learn that the key element is the yoke, namely the band of material that runs across the shoulder area and from which falls the body of the shirt. If this does not fit correctly then the rest of the garment won't either. While a couple of pleats are permitted on the back of the shirt (or a couple of darts for a more fitted style), the front should fall flat and fit snugly; the baggier the shirt, the less flattering to your frame. Breast pockets are problematic because they ruin the line of the shirt and so are best avoided; there are plenty of other places to store your glasses, credit cards, or phone.

As regards length, there needs to be enough fabric that the shirt will not pop out of your waistband, but not so much material that it bunches when tucked into pants. While the untucked shirt is popular in certain circles, it should not be encouraged, because the result invariably looks untidy. It also implies that the man in question has put on weight and is trying to disguise evidence of this by not showing his waistband.

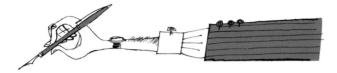

Sleeves and Cuffs

Sleeves should begin with armholes that fit well but are not so tight as to cut into the flesh, especially at the armpit. Likewise the main part of the sleeve should allow free movement but should not billow; when buying a new shirt it is worth seeing how it fits when worn beneath a sweater or jacket.

Sleeves should always be long enough to show sufficient cuff when hitting the wrist. In general, a cuff, whether single or double, should finish four and a half inches (11cm) from your thumb. When wearing any kind of jacket, approximately half an inch (1cm) of cuff must be visible.

In general, a cuff, whether single or double, should finish four and a half inches from your thumb

The standard, or barrel, cuff is made from a single band of fabric and has one or two buttons to fasten it at the wrist. The French, or double, cuff folds back on itself and is fastened with cuff links, which should be visible when fastened and worn beneath a jacket.

Short-sleeved shirts never look entirely agreeable, perhaps because they suggest insufficient fabric was available to the manufacturer. If you want to adopt a casual appearance, better to roll up your sleeves.

Collar Styles

Collars ought to fit but not to the point of threatening strangulation; ideally you should be able to fit two fingers under the collar at the side of the neck. The height and shape of the collar depend on taste but also on your own physique: a long neck, for example, responds better than does a short one to a high collar, especially one that fastens with a double button. Likewise the collar's shape will vary according to the size of tie-knot (or, indeed, lack of tie): As a rule, the wider the knot the more cutaway the collar. Unless wearing a button-down shirt, always use collar stays as they help to present a crisper appearance.

Among the commonly found collar styles is the Windsor, which is fairly widely spread—anything between four and six inches (10–15cm) between the collar points—and often found on business shirts. A narrower or smaller collar can look well but will only be able to accommodate thin ties.

The button-down collar is an American invention created by Brooks Brothers at the very end of the 19th century; it has not traveled much across the Atlantic because Europeans still prefer the Windsor collar. A variation of the button-down theme is the tab collar in which two narrow strips of fabric extend to the button point and are there linked behind a tie.

While most collars have pointed tips, occasionally one sees them with rounded ends: These are known as club collars. A shirt with a collar in a contrasting color to the main body of the shirt (most usually a white collar with striped body) is really a throwback to the days of the detachable collar. This style of shirt tends to be found in a business environment and looks out of place when worn without the accompaniment of a tie.

Fabric

Just as wool is by far the best fabric for suits, so cotton is ideal for shirting, with various forms of cotton poplin being most widely used for this purpose. Like wool, cotton is a natural material that is versatile, allows the skin to breathe, and takes and retains color well, but is also capable of surviving long-term use and regular washing.

Types of Weaves

A variety of weaves can be found in shirting cotton, the most ordinary being the plain weave where warp and weft (the horizontal and vertical threads combined to make cloth) are aligned to form a regular crisscross pattern. Oxford, which has a basketweave structure, provides a more hard-wearing weave than plain and so, too, does twill, which forms a pattern of diagonal parallel ribs by passing the weft over the warp thread. The twill weave's durability means it is also used for chino, denim, tweed, and gabardine. Satin weave imparts luster to the fabric and is therefore best kept for eveningwear shirts. Chambray is cotton woven with a colored warp and white weft, while flannelette is cotton that has been given a fur nap during the milling process to make it especially soft to the touch.

Alternatives to Cotton

Linen, which used to be the fabric of choice for gentlemen's shirts, is less widely used today except during summer months. It is vulnerable to wrinkling and can therefore quickly look untidy. Silk is the most luxurious of shirting materials but no longer tends to be much deployed for this purpose, except on occasion for eveningwear; even in heavier shantung, it is really too fine a fabric for day shirts.

Colors and Patterns

Every gentleman's wardrobe ought to hold several plain white shirts in various weights and weaves, all kept in pristine condition. You will find the white shirt invaluable, not least because it possesses universal adaptability to changing circumstances: A good white shirt looks as well with a suit as it does with jeans. Do not fret that a monochromatic shirt need be dull. There will be plenty of surface texture when it has been made with an Oxford or twill weave. Therefore, if you are planning to spend a reasonable sum of money on a couple of shirts, it is best to choose white. You will find they repay the investment.

As regards other colors, almost all are possible, but you ought to take your skin tone into account and be aware that not every shade will necessarily look well next to your face. As a general rule, during the daytime paler shades will suit you better, with darker ones kept for evenings. Likewise shirt patterns offer you an opportunity to play around with your wardrobe, although again a degree of moderation is recommended. Stripes look well in a business setting, as can some gingham, provided it is literally held in check. Other patterns, such as paisley, are best kept for informal times since they can very quickly impart the impression of frivolity to your appearance.

Don't be afraid to play around with your shirts, but, at the same time, bear in mind that mistakes can easily be made, especially if you are insufficiently aware of what best suits you and your style of dress.

Looking After Your Shirt

You should change your shirt, like your underwear, at least once a day. If you have an engagement in the evening, it is best to wear a clean shirt (and to shower before putting it on). Cotton is a resilient material and shirts can be washed in moderately hot water in order to make sure they are thoroughly cleaned; beforehand it is worth applying a specific stain removing detergent around the cuffs and collar as these areas are most vulnerable to dirt.

Never wash shirts in too hot a temperature as it may cause the fibers to shrink and the color to fade. Inevitably both shrinkage and fading are liable to happen over time, but there is no point in speeding up the process.

Avoiding Wrinkles

Hang the shirts to dry and iron them while they are still slightly damp as this will help to produce a smoother finish. In any case, you ought to use a steam iron for this purpose (or, alternatively, have close to hand a spray bottle filled with water). For a sharper look, use a spray starch on the sleeves and main body of the shirt (not on the collar as this could irritate your neck). When finished, hang your shirt again, with the top button closed to hold it in place. After a few hours, when it is completely dry, you can fold and store it away.

Try not to stack too many shirts on top of each other, because this might result in unwelcome wrinkling. Ideally, you should shake out a shirt and hang it up the night before it is being worn; this will reduce the wrinkles. Incidentally, the old trick of removing wrinkles by hanging a shirt within the steam of a hot running shower is still valid and particularly useful when you are traveling and without access to an iron.

Chapter 4

Knitwear

It is only in the past hundred years that knitwear has become a visible part of any gentleman's wardrobe. Previously, while a knitted garment might have been permissible when engaging in sport or as underwear, it was not usually worn in a social context. After World War I, however, long-established sartorial rules started to relax.

———◆◆———

In the 1920s knitted waistcoats became fashionable and, in particular, the trend-setting Prince of Wales (later Duke of Windsor) took to wearing knitted tops in a Fair Isle pattern while playing golf: hence their rise in acceptability. Nevertheless, note how the association with sport still remained, as it did with V-neck sweaters carrying a particular sporting club's colors around the neck and hem. Only in the 1930s did knitwear make the full transition from sports arena to everyday environment. Even so, it was very much a casual style, meant to be worn only inside the home and on informal occasions.

Sleeveless sweaters worn with tweed jackets became popular, as did V-necks with the diamond pattern known as Argyle. It took another world war before crewneck and turtleneck sweaters, known as polo-necks in the UK, began to be seen in public, initially worn by a generation of avant-garde artists and musicians before being taken up by the general population. Cardigans likewise gradually grew in popularity during the postwar decades. By the 1960s knitwear had become entirely mainstream, taken up by designers such as the Italians Tai and Rosita Missoni who gave sweaters a fashion fillip. So it remains to this day and now every gentleman is likely to own a number of pieces of knitwear. At all times it serves a dual purpose: to provide warmth and to add style. If either of these functions is not met, then the knit in question has not done its job.

Choosing Materials

Different animal fibers can be used in the manufacture of knitwear, the most widespread being lamb's-wool. Sheared from sheep up to seven months old, it is light in weight and easy to spin into yarn.

Cashmere is taken from the coat of a goat of the same name and is a byword for comfort

The Merino sheep is agreed to produce some of the very finest and softest wool, while Shetland sheep yield wool that is inclined to be coarse but resilient. There are various other yarns used in knitwear such as vicuña and alpaca, both of which are taken from species of South American llama and are renowned for their luxurious softness. So, too, is angora, which comes from a species of rabbit bred since the 18th century for this purpose. Cashmere is taken from the coat of a goat of the same name and is a byword for comfort and cost, not surprisingly since the average annual yield per goat is only five ounces (around 150 grams). Cashmere manages to be both light and warm, and this combination—when added to its inherently tactile qualities—explains the fiber's abiding popularity in the manufacture of quality knitwear. Any and all of these natural fibers are acceptable for knitwear. Artificial fibers are not.

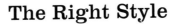

The Right Style

What style knitwear you choose depends on both the occasion and your own physique.

Sweaters are still predominantly associated with informality and rarely seen in the average workplace. Therefore they are not, as a rule, worn with suits. However, if you are going to do so you will find your jacket's shape is least disrupted by the inclusion of a lightweight sleeveless top; bulkier items will distort the whole profile. In some creative professions, crewnecks and turtlenecks are found worn with suits; again, lighter weights will work best.

Outside the office, at the weekend, and on vacation you should choose a style that best suits your body shape. A V-neck sweater will elongate the torso, especially if it has vertical bands incorporated into the knit. It is therefore flattering to short men. If you have a long, thin neck then the crewneck—which has a round neckline finishing well below the Adam's apple—will not be especially flattering. On the other hand, a turtleneck (which is useful for concealing the wrinkly skin of this area) should be avoided by men with short necks as it only emphasizes this aspect of their physiology.

Advice on Fit

Your knitwear ought to fit comfortably but properly. As with suit jackets, many men are inclined to wear sweaters too big for them, with the result that they look untidy. Avoid knitwear that bags at the midriff, otherwise it will give the erroneous impression that you have a paunch. On the other hand, if you are somewhat thickset, don't wear a tight sweater: the outline of your stomach straining to escape its confines will not win admirers. Men carrying additional weight should consider cardigans since these have the merit of being left partially or wholly unbuttoned.

*Do regard knitwear as an opportunity
of introducing color into your dress*

Acceptable Patterns

Aside from classic Fair Isle and Argyle, it is recommended that you steer well clear of patterns in knitwear; novelty in this area is rarely carried off with élan (remember Colin Firth's seasonal Christmas sweater in *Bridget Jones's Diary*?). The merit of vertical stripes has already been mentioned. Horizontal stripes can likewise deceive the eye, in this instance by making a thin man look broader, although with some knitwear they can also make him look like an aspiring French sailor. Within reasonable boundaries, do regard knitwear as an opportunity of introducing color into your dress, especially if the rest of your outfit is sober in design and cut.

Caring For Your Garment

The natural fibers used in its construction mean that all knitwear will stretch somewhat when worn—and correspondingly shrink when washed. Learn how to take off your knitwear properly (that is, using two hands and from the bottom waistband up over your head) as this will preserve its shape better. Always fold your sweater after use, preferably incorporating tissue paper. All knitwear should be washed, ideally by hand and at a low temperature, before being laid flat to dry. Never tumble dry your sweaters as this will cause the fibers to shrink and will distort the garment's shape.

Chapter 5

Ties

Even though today it serves no practical purpose, the tie remains an essential element in any gentleman's wardrobe. In its present guise this item of clothing can be traced back to the cravats worn by men from the mid-17th century onward; these took the place of ruffs, which had previously been the preferred style of neck attire. Over the next 150-odd years cravats changed from an elaborate confection of lace to a simple folded piece of white linen carefully knotted below the chin. A version of this survives to the present day in the form of the stock worn by horsemen when out hunting.

———◆———

The elegance of the cravat reached its peak in the early 1800s: Regency dandy Beau Brummell is supposed to have spent entire mornings perfecting the finish of his cravat before he was ready to emerge from his home. However, during the second half of the 19th century the cravat in turn began to be superseded by the tie as we now know it: a plain strip of fabric wound once around the neck and then tied in a knot at the front from which two ends descend toward the waist.

What Your Tie Says about You

The tie has come to have an unexpected function, its objective being not to keep the body warm but to send out a signal about the wearer's place in society. Essentially ties are symbols, not least of conformity—hence an inevitable reluctance on the part of the young and would-be rebellious to wear them. Hence, too, the popularity of ties carrying emblems or crests, or particular sequences of stripes: These indicate the wearer is a member of a specific group or club. The phrase "old school tie" has become a figure of speech denoting the merits of belonging to a particular caste. In addition, ties are deemed to signify respectability, making them a requisite feature of business dress. Ties are not easy to produce and are complex works of engineering that should be admired. Finally, ties have developed in line with the modern suit and shirt, and therefore naturally harmonize with them. For all these reasons, you ought to have a number of ties in your wardrobe.

Fabric Selection

As a rule ties are made of silk and certainly no synthetic materials should be used to produce them. The silk must be woven and it is easy to detect whether this is the case by looking at a tie's pattern, which ought never to be printed. Different weights and weaves of silk—such as twill and poplin—will produce varying styles of material for use in a tie and this in turn has an impact on the knot used when tying it. Bear in mind these factors when purchasing a tie. For a more relaxed approach, consider knitted ties, either in silk or cashmere. These work well in rural environments when combined with a sleeveless sweater and tweed jacket; in such scenarios a woven silk tie can look too urban.

Color and Pattern

Ties permit a man to express something of his personality even when the rest of what he is wearing suggests anonymous uniformity. For this reason, you need not shirk away from bold colors and patterns, provided they complement rather than conflict with your shirt and suit. Relish the opportunity to demonstrate individual taste through your choice of tie while remaining within the bounds of good taste. Think in terms of classic designs like diagonal stripes or paisley patterns rather than novelty. Avoid "jokey" ties or anything intended to be funny, or the laugh will inevitably be on you. And obviously you should never wear a tie connected with any institution, such as a club or school, unless you really have links with it.

Tying Your Tie

In Oscar Wilde's 1893 play *A Woman of No Importance*, the droll Lord Illingworth proclaims, "A well-tied tie is the first serious step in life." It transpires there are a surprisingly large number of ways to tie a tie. In 1999, two Cambridge University physicists, Thomas Fink and Yong Mao, published a book called *The 85 Ways to Tie a Tie: The Science and Aesthetics of Tie Knots* in which they listed all the possible ways of tying a tie, but then picked out thirteen, including four classics—the four-in-hand, the Pratt, the half-Windsor, and the Windsor—which stood out as aesthetically satisfying. Most men tend to use the four-in-hand, which is relatively easy to learn and also looks well with all widths and weights of fabric. The Windsor dates from the 1930s and takes its name from the Duke of Windsor, who then liked a broad knot; the half-Windsor is a variation on this theme.

Correct Length

If you prefer to learn how to tie a variety of knots such as the Windsor and half-Windsor, several websites offer guidance on the subject and provide helpful illustrations for each stage of the process.

Be careful to wear your tie neither too long nor too short: It should stop just short of your belt. The narrower tail should be concealed behind the front and if there is a loop at the rear of the latter use this to tuck away the former. Clip-on ties, obviously, are never to be countenanced.

Looking After Your Ties

As with the rest of your wardrobe, if you take care of a tie you will find it gives longer and better service. Never wear a tie on consecutive days but allow at least 24 hours for it to recover its shape. Ideally you should not hang your ties (most especially if they are knitted) but roll them up from the thin end and then store them flat. If you must hang your tie collection, buy a hanger designed for this function. To remove wrinkles in a tie, hold it up before the steam of a kettle (making sure the entire item does not become wet). Avoid ironing ties because it often flattens the natural bounce of the fabric used in their manufacture.

Ties are prone to become stained, particularly with food. These marks should be removed as soon as possible, preferably with an appropriate spot remover. Test the product's efficacy and potential risk to the fabric beforehand, using an inconspicuous section of the tie at the back. Always dab a stain rather than rubbing it which could affect the color of the material. Likewise do not wash ties since the nature of their construction (more complicated than you might imagine) is likely to mean different sections have different shrink rates.

How to Tie a Four-in-Hand

1. 1. A four-in-hand is very straightforward. Start by hanging the tie around your neck with the widest section to the right and falling longer than the narrow part.

2. Pass the wide end over the front of the narrow end to the left, then under it to the right.

3. Pass the wide end over the front of the narrow end to the left once more.

4. Now pass the wide end behind the semi-formed knot and pull it up toward your chin.

5. Finally, pass the wide end between the outer layer of the knot and the layer directly behind it, before pulling the tip of the tie through.

6. Hold the narrow end firmly and then tighten the knot until it is sitting firmly but comfortably at the top of your shirt.

Bow Ties

 The bow tie is a prerequisite of evening dress. In recent years some men have taken to wearing a regular knotted black tie in its place but this makes a very poor second, rather like serving sparkling wine instead of Champagne. If you are wearing the full formality of evening tails, then the bow tie, like your wing-collared shirt, ought to be made of white cotton piqué. When donning a tuxedo, or dinner jacket, your tie will be of black ribbed silk. Colored ties in the evening are a sartorial solecism made even worse when they are accompanied by matching cummerbunds or waistcoats. Evening bow ties must always be either white or black, depending on the circumstances; nothing else is acceptable.

Sadly, few men now wear bow ties during the day and they are certainly not part of contemporary business attire, as was the case even until half a century ago. With a tweed jacket or a cardigan, a paisley pattern bow tie can provide a nice touch, intimating a kind of relaxed formality. For daywear, patterned rather than plain bows are indubitably preferable and suggestive of an earlier, less frenetic era than our own.

Does it need to be said that pre-tied bows are absolutely beyond the pale? It is astonishing how many men who regard themselves as practical and competent to change a tire or investigate the intricacies of computer components are rendered helpless when required to tie a bow around their necks. As a means of enticing a woman to stand immediately behind and put her arms around you, this display of dependency has a certain charm but what if there is no such woman around? As with other aspects of adulthood, self-reliance is required when it comes to tying a bow.

How to Tie a Bow Tie

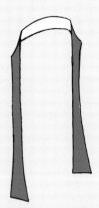

1. Drape the tie around your neck leaving one end an inch or two longer than the other.

2. Cross the longer end over the shorter end.

3. Using the longer end, wrap it around the shorter end and tie a simple knot.

4. Hold up the longer end with your thumb and forefinger by your face so that it is out of the way. With your other hand, form the short end into a bow.

5. Let the longer end fall down over the front of the bow, which you must now hold in position. Grasp the longer end and force half of it through the gap which is behind the bow.

6. After pushing the bow through from one side, pull on the other side and thus tighten the knot before straightening all the layers so that they form a neat bow. If any part is longer than the rest or skewed, gently tug or twist it so that the whole tie looks neat.

Chapter 6

Shoes

It used to be said that hotel concierges could judge the financial status of their guests by the condition of the latter's shoes: The scruffier their footwear, the less they were deemed to be worth (and therefore liable to receive a proportionately poorer reception). But the casual shoes favored by many of today's new billionaires give no indication of their immense wealth, so that rule has had to be discarded.

———◆———

Even if you can no longer estimate the size of a man's bank balance by how he is shod, you can still gain a fair understanding of how much pride he takes in himself and his appearance by the state of his shoes. Scruffy footwear suggests a slovenly attitude. A pair of clean, well-polished shoes, on the other hand, indicates orderliness and an appreciation of standards.

Getting the Right Size

It is worth spending as much as you can on your shoes, not least because they offer vital support as you walk and stand your way through the average day. Rather like the bespoke suit, if your bank balance allows you to commission a pair of custom-made shoes, then you should do so. Constructed to fit you like a second skin, with due maintenance they will last the rest of your lifetime. Should such expenditure be beyond your means, at least take the trouble to have your feet correctly measured and thereafter only buy shoes that are the right size. Disregard any sales assistant who assures you a shoe will stretch or become softer with wear—it ought to be comfortable from the first occasion.

Most men find that their right foot is fractionally larger than the left, so always try on the right shoe first. If it fits properly, more than likely so too will the left. Always scrupulously examine shoes before you buy them, paying particular attention to how well the uppers and soles have been stitched together since this is often an area where standards are allowed to slip.

Acceptable Materials

Other than sports shoes and sneakers, all your shoes must be made of an animal hide, most commonly calf although there is also a rich leather called Cordovan made from the flat muscle beneath the hide on a horse's rump. Hide will respond best to your own skin, subtly expanding and contracting as do the feet they encase, allowing your feet to breathe and absorbing any excess perspiration that passes through the hide before being dispersed into the outside air. Occasionally other hides, such as buckskin (from deer) and those taken from reptiles or birds like ostrich, are used for the manufacture of shoes, but the result is inclined to be rather flashy and attention-seeking.

Leather or Suede?

Until the 1920s suede was viewed with suspicion but then, as in so many other areas of men's fashion, it was espoused by the future Duke of Windsor and thus acquired a degree of respectability. Leather tends to look better in a formal or professional environment, while suede is more suited to casual times like weekends at home. Patent leather should only be used for evening shoes.

Leather tends to look better in a formal or professional environment, while suede is more suited to casual times

Black or Brown?

It used to be a strict rule that gentlemen never wore brown shoes in town; they were kept for the country. However, this no longer applies. Paradoxically, black shoes often look out of place in a rural setting, so keep brown shoes to hand (or rather, to foot) whenever in the countryside. Ideally your wardrobe should contain several pairs of shoes in both colors.

Can you wear shoes of a color other than black or brown? Certainly not in leather, but a colored suede can look stylish for casual loafers, especially in warmer climates.

A Style to Suit the Occasion

The Oxford is the stalwart of shoes, a basic, plain style characterized by the way in which the lace eyelets are stitched beneath the upper (or vamp, as it is known). The Derby, on the other hand, has its lace eyelets stitched on top of the vamp.

The wing-tip is distinguished from the Oxford by the shape of the toe cap which instead of running straight across the bridge of the shoe spreads in a fashion not unlike that of the open wings of a bird.

Oxfords work well with a business suit and are certainly the preferred style in a professional environment.

Brogues can be worn with a business suit but as befits their Scottish origins look exceptionally well with tweeds

The brogue originated in the Scottish Highlands and is identifiable by the elaborate series of tiny holes punched across sections of the shoe upper which is also decorated with double-stitched seams. The difference between a half- and a full-brogue is that the former's perforation and double-stitching are confined to the front section of the shoe. Brogues can be worn with a business suit but as befits their Scottish origins look exceptionally well with tweeds.

The monk shoe does not have laces but instead a strap passes across the instep and is fastened by a buckle. It is the descendant of the 17th-century buckled shoe but only emerged in its present form in the 1930s. The monk shoe is extremely versatile and combines well with both formal and casual clothes.

The loafer (or moccasin) likewise first appeared during the 1930s and originated in Norway where it was made by fishermen. Obviously at first it was a somewhat rough-and-ready product but soon underwent refinement in accordance with increased popularity. It now comes in several variants such as the tassel loafer, the kiltie (which has a fringe across the instep), and the penny-loafer, so called because during the 1950s there was a fad for lodging pennies in the little diamond-shaped cutout at the top. In the mid-1960s Gucci added a metal strap across the front of its loafers in the shape of a horse's snaffle bit and this has since been much emulated. Loafers, depending on their style and finish, are sufficiently adaptable to be worn in almost every circumstance.

> *Loafers, depending on their style and finish, are sufficiently adaptable to be worn in almost every circumstance*

The boat or deck shoe, as its name indicates, began life on board a seagoing vessel where the combination of nonslip soles and water-repellent leather made it invaluable. No longer confined offshore, deck shoes are now found on land but are strictly for casualwear.

The pump is a shoe designed for evening wear. It is entirely plain and low-heeled, made from either polished or patent hide and most commonly is slip-on.

Chelsea boots are really the only kind of boots that can be worn when not playing sport. They derive from a 19th-century fitted, ankle-high jodhpur boot and have elasticized sidings. In the 1960s they became highly fashionable and have remained popular ever since. They are casual items and not suited to the workplace.

Looking After Your Shoes

There is no reason why a pair of shoes should not continue to provide sturdy service for many years—no reason other than your failure to take as much care of them as they have of you. Follow these rules to keep your shoes in a good state of repair:

✱ Never wear shoes on consecutive days. Allow them to rest and recover from being worn.

✱ Always use shoe trees when they are resting as this will help immeasurably in preserving their correct shape.

✱ If your shoes get wet, stuff them with newspaper which will absorb the excess moisture. Change the paper a couple of times to make sure all the water has been soaked up.

✱ Regularly check the heels of your shoes and have the rubber of these replaced as soon as it starts to show evidence of being worn down. Likewise the soles will need to be periodically repaired.

✱ When traveling, pack your shoes inside individual shoe bags. This will ensure they do not get scratched or leave marks on other items.

✱ Above all, clean and polish your shoes on a weekly basis using a cream polish, which will nourish and protect the leather. Ideally you should apply the polish and then leave it for a while to be absorbed into the shoe before buffing it to a high sheen. Any dirt should be removed beforehand with a damp sponge.

✱ Suede shoes can also be maintained with the aid of a brush intended for this purpose, using short strokes in the direction of the nap to remove any dirt.

*Clean and polish your shoes on a weekly basis
using a cream polish, which will nourish
and protect the leather*

Chapter 7

Socks and Underwear

Just because it's not on public view, you shouldn't assume the state of your underwear is unimportant. The female equivalent used to be known as foundation garments, and that's how you should view these items: as providing a sound base for your clothes. Likewise young girls were once told by their mothers always to wear clean underwear in case they were hit by a bus and taken to hospital. You needn't imagine such a drastic scene but there will come times when you're grateful to have put on decent underwear that day.

———◆———

Socks

All of us have an abundance of socks in our wardrobe, ideally kept in matching pairs: The riddle of the missing sock will be familiar to every man and defies explanation. There are really only a handful of rules to follow when it comes to these items, and none is too arduous.

Fabrics used for the making of socks were once entirely natural, such as silk, cashmere, wool, and cotton. These are still employed but most often today mixed with a certain percentage of a man-made material like polyamide, which greatly increases the durability of the finished item.

This is especially important for socks which can otherwise suffer the affliction of becoming speedily worn out and then ruined by the emergence of holes at heel and toe. So for once a degree of man-made fiber is to be recommended, but not more than 20 percent.

The riddle of the missing sock will be familiar to every man and defies explanation

Silk is best for evening socks, being lighter and finer; cashmere is especially luxurious (but not terribly hard-wearing); wool is generally warmer than cotton, the latter being best kept for summer socks. Merino wool is the ideal for everyday socks.

Colored and patterned socks can enhance an outfit provided they harmonize with it and do not upstage it

Color and Pattern

For office and formal occasions, your socks will be dark and without any knitted ribbing. Ribbed socks are for weekends and sports attire.

Your socks should always be at least one shade darker than your trousers and, off the tennis court or sports field, ought never to be white. Colored and patterned socks can enhance an outfit provided they harmonize with what else is being worn and do not try to upstage it. Beware of novelty socks—you'll find the novelty wears out faster than the socks.

Sock Length

Wear a sock of sufficient length so that when you sit down no calf is exposed. There are few more unattractive spectacles than a band of pale flesh between bottom of pant leg and top of sock. Garters used to be needed in order to keep the top of a sock in place but elastication has done away with this; just make sure your socks retain their elasticity and do not end up crumpled around the ankle.

Looking After Your Socks

As with other knitwear, due care ought to be taken when washing socks. This is best done at a low temperature to avoid both shrinkage and color loss.

Regularly check your socks for holes: They can appear with startling ease and a man with a hole in his hosiery is a sorry sight. The days of sock mushrooms (used for darning repairs) are long over, but if you want to increase the chances of a sock's longevity, keep your toenails short and your ankle smooth. While it is impossible to guarantee against losing one half of a pair, the danger will be reduced if you fold the top of each set of socks over one another before putting them away.

Underwear

The function of underwear is first and foremost hygienic: to act as a protective layer between your body and its secretions and your outer garments. In cold weather it also provides a layer of warmth. Any other advantage is supplementary, so you should choose underwear for its ability to perform a sanitary function. This means, above all else, making sure it is made from a natural fiber, most commonly

cotton, although, as with socks, a small element of man-made fiber—such as Lycra—in the mix is permissible, not least because it ensures a snugger fit. Linen and silk are more expensive and do not necessarily do a better job than cotton. In an era of central heating, wool underwear is redundant. Men's underwear at the start of the 20th century was usually the one-piece set of long johns encasing an entire form from neck to wrist and ankle. This shrank and separated into two separate pieces, one for the upper body, one for the lower.

What style your underwear takes—briefs, boxers, fitted shorts—is a matter of personal predilection

Undershirts and T-shirts

The undershirt, or vest, which was widely worn during those early decades, suffered an irreversible decline in popularity after Clark Gable removed his shirt in the 1934 Frank Capra film *It Happened One Night* and revealed he was wearing nothing beneath. Thereafter undershirts have been afflicted with the notion that they are old-fashioned. Their place in a man's wardrobe has been largely supplanted by the T-shirt which was popularized in the 1950s by another film actor, Marlon Brando. While it may be tempting to dispense with anything beneath your shirt, wearing some kind of undershirt or T retains merit, not least because it will absorb the evidence should you perspire during the day.

Boxers or Briefs?

Some men are likewise attracted to the notion of going "commando," that is, not bothering with any lower underwear. For reasons of hygiene this is to be discouraged. What style your underwear takes—briefs, boxers, fitted shorts—is a matter of personal predilection since it is unlikely to be seen by the majority of people you meet. It has sometimes been proposed that a man's fecundity can be adversely affected by too-tight clothing, but there is no absolute evidence proving this to be so. Ultimately, comfort ought to be your guide. Plain colors and an absence of pattern are probably preferable, but if you want to use your underwear as an opportunity to express individuality it has the advantage of being a discreet manifestation.

What can absolutely not be disputed is the importance of keeping your underwear clean and changing it at least once a day. Under no circumstances can this rule be breached.

Chapter 8

Accessories

Accessories are finishing touches, not critical to your overall appearance but capable of lifting you from the realm of smartly dressed to the heights of impeccably turned out. Remember that it's the little things that make all the difference and accessorize accordingly.

————•————

Hats

The reason for the disappearance of the hat from a gentleman's wardrobe during the second half of the last century is a mystery that cannot be solved. To some extent it had to do with increased informality: Until around 1950 no man with aspirations to gentility would think of being seen in public without a hat, which he would remove both when meeting a woman and when entering a building. Thus the wearing of a hat was associated in the popular mind with traditional social etiquette and as this fell out of favor so did all those items of clothing with which it was linked.

But hats also serve a practical function, namely to retain the head's heat or, in warmer climes, to provide necessary protection from the glare of the sun. It is estimated that below certain temperatures some 25 percent of our body heat is lost through the uncovered head. Therefore, discarding the hat, far from being a gesture of progress, was actually a retrograde step. A bare head is an exposed head, and will suffer the consequences: In very hot countries the absence of a hat can even lead to sunstroke. It is hardly surprising that in recent years all sorts of headgear have become popular, especially during winter months and among the young. Once temperatures begin to drop, almost everyone wears something on his head, the only difference from earlier times being that today we don't all opt for the same kind of covering.

If you are going to wear a hat, make sure it fits properly: It should sit in place comfortably and securely, neither too tight nor too loose. It is worth having your head measured by a hatter in order to know your correct size for future purchases. Also, given that specific styles are no longer obligatory, be aware of what best suits your head and features, something that can really only be discovered by trial and error.

Types of Hats

The harder and more inflexible the hat, the greater the formality of the occasion. Therefore the most formal of all is the silk top hat, which made its appearance in the closing decades of the 18th century when it displaced the three-cornered hat, or tricorne. Initially worn by all classes and at all times of day, from the middle of the 19th century onward it came to be associated with formal wear and that remains the case to this day. Black silk top hats are now only seen with tails and white tie. More commonly worn in Britain is the gray top hat, made of gray fur felt and accompanying a morning suit on such occasions as weddings, or a smart race meeting like Royal Ascot.

One of the reasons for the decline of the top hat's prevalence from 1850 onward was the rise of the Bowler. Named after its designers, Thomas and William Bowler, it made its debut around that time after a customer of the London hatters James Lock & Co commissioned a close-fitting, low-crowned hat to protect gamekeepers' heads while on horseback. The gray version is known as the Derby, after the 17th Earl of Derby who wore such a style at a race meeting. In the early 20th century the Bowler was ubiquitous, especially as the hat of choice for executives. It survived World War II but then went into a decline and today is pretty much an anachronism.

Other felt hats have survived somewhat better, including the Homburg, which was popularized by Britain's King Edward VII when Prince of Wales. It has a fixed shape with a dent in the crown running from back to front, and a brim bound with ribbon and curving up at the sides. The Trilby—named after the eponymous heroine of George du Maurier's 1894 novel—has a similar dent in the crown but is softer with a wider, unbound brim. The Borsalino, made by an Italian firm of the same name established in 1857, is similar in form with a triangular pinch to the crown.

The Panama is similar in shape to the Trilby but made traditionally in Ecuador from the plaited leaves of the toquilla straw plant. While other hats fell from favor, somehow the Panama always retained its popularity, perhaps because it is both practical and informal. It also manages to look well even when somewhat aged and battered. On the other hand the boater, which is made of a stiff woven straw, is irretrievably associated with an earlier era; outside period films and television dramas it is unlikely to experience a revival.

There is a huge selection of tweed hats and caps now on the market. These are fine with casual clothes and sportcoat but not really suitable as accompaniment for workplace or formal attire. Similarly, woolen hats, baseball caps, and so forth are strictly for informal occasions.

Gloves

Like hats, gloves used to be an everyday part of the gentleman's wardrobe. They were worn on almost every occasion: when either riding or walking in public, as well as at the theater or going to church. One of the functions of gloves in earlier times was the protection of hands, both from the cold and from dirt and germs. They can still serve the same purpose and ought to remain an integral part of your daily wardrobe, except, of course, when the weather grows too warm.

Acceptable Materials

In winter, for heat it is recommended that you wear gloves lined in cashmere, which has the advantage of being deliciously soft. In spring, change these for gloves lined in silk.

Your gloves should be of the finest leather affordable. Originating from South American wild hogs, peccary is the rarest and most luxurious leather used for gloves. More normally hair-sheep leather—which, as its name indicates, comes from sheep that grow hair rather than wool—is employed, because it combines suppleness and strength with softness. Deerskin is especially tough but it is heavier and more rugged in appearance. Cheaper gloves are often made from cowhide and goatskin.

Caring for Your Gloves

As with every other item in your wardrobe, be sure to buy gloves in the right size. Too small and they will pinch, too big and they will not necessarily keep your hands as warm as ought to be the case.

Just like the hands they contain, gloves suffer from rough treatment and benefit from care. After a day's wear, always gently stretch each finger and the main body to restore its original shape. Lay the gloves flat, and store them in a dry place (damp will cause them to develop mold) and inside a cloth cover. Lightly sponge them with a moist cloth to remove any dirt and periodically treat them with something that will improve the leather and keep it supple; even petroleum jelly or a waterless hand moisturizer will serve the purpose. Rub this into the leather while wearing the gloves and then wipe off any excess with a dry cloth.

Umbrellas

The umbrella serves an entirely practical purpose but that does not mean it should not also be aesthetically pleasing. Initially an object of ridicule when it first made an appearance in 18th-century England, the umbrella proved so useful that it became an invaluable accessory, particularly in damper climes. Toward the close of the 19th century, a tightly rolled umbrella had begun to replace the walking stick as the object carried by every respectable gentleman.

Black is the only acceptable color for umbrella fabric

In an urban setting, a plain black umbrella remains the best choice, preferably one with a simple handle of stainless steel topped by either polished wood or stitched leather. Black is the only acceptable color for umbrella fabric. Until the 1940s this used to be made of fine silk, which was subject to discoloration and rotting when damp. Since then, however, a number of durable nylons have been developed and have now largely replaced silk. The collapsible, tote-style umbrella is extremely useful as it does not take up as much space, but is often of inferior manufacture and not as robust as the more traditional stick.

Golf umbrellas belong on the golf course; in towns and cities they take up too much room on the sidewalk and anyone carrying one in these places shows a selfish lack of consideration for his fellow men and women. Umbrellas displaying slogans or advertisements turn their owners into walking billboards.

If you have used your umbrella in the rain, always open it when you get home and allow the body to dry out before furling it up again. This will ensure a longer life for the item.

Jewelry

As far as men and jewelry are concerned, less is definitely best. Anything you wear should be simple in form and design, with minimal decoration and no overt evidence of expense.

With regard to rings, a plain band in gold or platinum on the third finger of your left hand is permissible as a statement of marriage. If you have a family crest, a gold signet ring may be worn on the little finger of the left hand: the seal should face outward to enable a wax impression to be taken without removing the ring. No other rings should be worn.

Any jewelry that involves piercing the flesh is not permissible. Likewise all bracelets and necklaces.

Cuff Links and Tie Pins

For double-cuff shirts, cuff links are a necessity. Once more they should be made of a precious metal, most often silver or gold, and should be as unostentatious as possible. The classic link involves two bars or studs linked by a chain but the alternative link by bar is also fine. With evening wear, links incorporating gems can look well, provided the stones are not too big. Cuff links made from colored silk knots can be worn with a shirt during the day, but precious metals are preferable at night. It is worth building up a small collection of links, to vary according to circumstance.

Shirt studs, again sometimes incorporating gems but more often with black enameled fronts, are deemed perfectly respectable with evening dress.

Tie pins and clips used to be in common usage but are not much seen today. Older examples often featured gemstones or enameled images but these now look unnecessarily fussy. If you are going to use something to keep your tie in place, make it as low-key as possible.

A Simple Timepiece

Your watch, like your shoes, provides information about you and your character. A cheap watch will make you look cheap. On the other hand, showiness here is to be avoided; although your watch might have cost a great deal of money, this should not be apparent. So no loud diamonds, no superfluous dials and buttons, no heavily ornamented wrist bands (the last of these should be in plain dark leather). Leave ostentation to drug dealers and rap stars, and let quiet good taste be your guiding principle in the selection of a watch and indeed all other pieces of jewelry.

When choosing a watch, showiness is to be avoided and cost should not be apparent. Leave ostentation to drug dealers and rap stars

Handkerchiefs

Whenever you get dressed, your finished ensemble should include two handkerchiefs, each serving a different function.

In your pants pocket you will carry a cotton handkerchief. This will be used for wiping or blowing your nose, as well as for mopping up any unexpected liquid spills, polishing your glasses, and so forth. Your pocket handkerchief should be changed regularly, at least once a day if you are suffering from a cold. While paper handkerchiefs are certainly practical, they are not very aesthetically appealing and are also inclined to disintegrate after minimal usage, necessitating their disposal. A cotton handkerchief is much more satisfactory and infinitely more desirable. Pocket handkerchiefs should always be of either cotton or linen and can be either plain white or patterned; a check or polka dot can be fun.

In contrast with this entirely practical item, your second handkerchief, tucked into the jacket breast pocket, will be strictly ornamental. The purpose of this handkerchief is to add decorative detail to what you are wearing, and very possibly a welcome burst of color, too. With regard to color and also pattern, these should complement whatever is already found in your tie and shirt but, if possible, not match them exactly: You should never be too coordinated, because this suggests a want of imagination and spontaneity, which are important elements in the appearance of any well-dressed gentleman. Having said that, a plain white handkerchief must be used for the breast pocket with evening wear.

The purpose of this handkerchief is to add decorative detail to what you are wearing, and very possibly a welcome burst of color, too

Wearing Your Handkerchief

How you place the handkerchief in your breast pocket depends on personal choice but will also be dictated by the fabric involved. Pure cotton and linen, for example, ought to be starched and are best worn in precise folds—either square-ended or else coming to a point as one or more triangles. Silk, and silk-mix, handkerchiefs in contrast look better when they have been puffed loosely in the hand and then inserted upside down into the breast pocket with the suggestion of informal flair.

Never leave a handkerchief in a jacket not being worn. Take it out and leave it neatly folded with other similar items.

Belts

Obviously the primary intent of a belt is to keep your pants from falling to the ground (as seen in a thousand comedy films), but they also help to complete an outfit, especially if the pants you are wearing have belt loops; in the absence of a belt these can look empty and gaping. Accordingly, you should always wear a belt if your pants are designed for this purpose.

The color of your belt should match that of your shoes and likewise be of leather. The belt's width should be in the region of an inch and a half (4cm) and its tongue should extend about three inches (7.5cm) beyond the buckle but not much more.

The color of your belt should match that of your shoes and likewise be of leather

For business and evening attire, a plain buckle is the only option acceptable. With casual pants and especially jeans, a decorative buckle can be worn—but keep the ornamentation within reasonable limits.

Suspenders

For a long time suspenders, known as braces in Britain, were much more popular than belts as a means of supporting men's pants. They were invented by the French around the time of the Revolution when knee breeches were abandoned for the more egalitarian trouser. High-waisted pants became fashionable in the early 19th century and a means had to be found to hold these up; hence the role of suspenders.

But in the 20th century, belts came to the fore, especially once the emergence of two-piece suits meant the abandonment of the waistcoat and the resultant exposure of suspenders, which were often more functional than elegant.

In the 1980s suspenders enjoyed a revival in popularity thanks to their appearance in films like *Wall Street*. It led to the illogical but widespread idea that there was some kind of association between this item of clothing and acquisition of financial acumen: All around the world would-be tycoons took to sporting suspenders. Since then they have once more reverted to possessing minority appeal but have never entirely been abandoned. Suspenders that are buttoned inside the pants waistband are more appealing than the clip-on variety since the former better conceal their utilitarianism. Suspenders should not be worn with pants that have belt loops. Wearing both suspenders and belt is like donning two hats or, indeed, two pairs of pants: a ludicrous sartorial solecism.

Chapter 9

Formal Occasions

By their nature formal occasions do not encourage spontaneity or expressions of individuality in matters of dress. There are well-established codes to be followed and unless you particularly yearn to be noticed it is best to adhere to them. Besides, as a demonstration of personal rebellion your failure to wear the correct clothes to a wedding can hardly be deemed radical. Better to adhere to the established rules and find another opportunity for a display of your seditious character.

———◆———

Evening Wear

While men have a limited choice of outfit for evening functions compared with women, there is still a margin for error when planning your outfit. Men's evening dress can be summarized as falling into two categories: the dresscoat and the tuxedo, also known as a dinner jacket. Consider carefully the purpose of the night's engagement and ensure that you dress appropriately.

The Dress Coat

The white tie dress code, also known as full evening dress, is, and has been for more than a century, the most formal style of male costume, worn only on grand occasions such as a formal ball or gala evening.

As such, its components are firmly regulated and do not admit of variation. The centerpiece of the ensemble is the black evening tailcoat—the dress coat—made of a lightweight mohair with silk facings, cut away horizontally at the front. The reason for this style lies in its late 18th-century origins, when a coat was needed that could be worn by men when riding. In its current incarnation, the dress coat is a descendant of an item once worn during both day and night toward the close of the 18th century. For day wear it was supplanted around the middle of the 19th century by the frock coat and this in turn gave way to the morning coat, which is still worn today for some government and civic events. In Britain and Europe it is also worn at formal weddings and so forth. In the Regency era, trousers or breeches did not match the dress coat, but since the latter became exclusively the preserve of evening wear, it has been customary for both to be made from the same cloth, and always to be black.

The dress coat is, and has been for more than a century, the most formal style of male costume

In cut, the coat is waist-length at front and sides, but at the rear has two long swallowtails falling to the knee. Remember them before sitting down—rather than crushing them on the seat, you should separate the tails, one to either side of your chair. Since the 1870s the coat has been double-breasted with two rows of buttons. However, these are only decorative as the coat does not fasten. Unlike its ancestor, it has no external pockets other than one at the breast.

The accompanying pants, in the same fabric, will have a fish-tail back, indicating that they are to be held in place by suspenders (known as braces in Britain) rather than a belt. Down the outer seams runs a single or double stripe of silk braid.

Your shirt will be plain white with a stiff front of cotton piqué and a wing collar. This will be accompanied by a white bow tie, also of cotton piqué. No other color should be countenanced. Likewise the waistcoat will be of white cotton piqué, cut low and double-breasted with a slim shawl collar. Its bottom should not extend lower than does the front of your dress coat, in order to present an unbroken black silhouette.

An evening shirt will be plain white and will be accompanied by a white bow tie. No other color is acceptable

Socks will be to the knee and black, preferably silk or else fine merino wool. Your footwear will likewise be black and if possible patent leather. Should you find yourself much in demand for formal evening occasions, it is worth acquiring a pair of plain black pumps (also known as court shoes) with bows of grossgrain. The only other accessories permissible are a plain white linen handkerchief in the breast pocket and/or a boutonniere in your buttonhole. Men in possession of military medals and other similar decorations also wear them on their dress coats. Every now and then someone will appear with a top hat which is also a traditional part of formal evening wear but rarely seen today. If you intend to carry one, it should be black, made of silk, and collapsible—a relic from the days when gentlemen wore such hats to the opera and had to store them under their chair. A dark coat and gloves, together with silk scarf, should be worn for protection of your clothes if you are traveling.

The Dinner Jacket

Although the dinner jacket is called a tuxedo in North America, the word tuxedo is also often used there for any tailcoat, so the term dinner jacket is used here to distinguish between them. It is worn for evening events where the dress code is black tie.

The dinner jacket is of far more recent vintage than the dress coat and its rise testifies to the increasingly casual nature of men's clothing over the past century. The dinner jacket can be traced back to a visit made in 1886 by the wealthy New Yorker James Potter to the Prince of Wales (later Edward VII) at Sandringham, England. Seemingly when Potter asked his host about a dresscode he was sent to the London tailor Henry Poole & Co, who provided him with a suit similar to the smoking jackets made to the Prince's specifications for the past quarter-century; this was, in effect, a dinner jacket and trousers. Returning to the United States, Potter wore his dinner suit to the club attached to Tuxedo Park, then one of New York's most fashionable residential districts. It quickly acquired a following among the club's members and from this derives its American name, the tuxedo.

The rise of the dinner jacket testifies to the increasingly casual nature of men's clothing over the last century

Initially, dinner jackets were seen only at home or in a club setting, while the dress coat continued to be worn on more public and formal occasions. However, from the 1920s onward it began to replace the dress coat and is now the standard male option for evening dress. Although open to a certain degree of flexibility, nevertheless some rules are best applied when wearing a dinner jacket. The classic style for jackets is that they be made of light mohair with ribbed satin facings on a shawl lapel (derived from smoking jackets) or peaked lapel (from

dress coats). Either single- or double-breasted is acceptable but the latter will accentuate any excess weight so only the slim should choose this style. Jackets should be either black or blue-black. If you wear another color, usually in velvet, it is classified as a smoking jacket, which in full fig will have a shawl collar and be fastened by silk froggings. Smoking jackets, while perfectly fine for a semiformal dinner in a private house, should not be worn to a public occasion.

The white dinner jacket originated in hot climates and traditionally was never seen in England: for a long time men who wore such a garment outside the tropics were regarded with suspicion. Although this is no longer the case, a white jacket will best be kept for summer evenings. Its color is not so much white as a pale ivory and it has a lapel, usually shawl, made of the same light fabric.

Regardless of the color of your jacket, the accompanying pants should always be black and made from light mohair with a single silk or satin braid running the length of the outer seams. Traditionally the pants are flat-fronted (that is, without pleats) and held in place by suspenders (braces), which are then concealed either by a waistcoat or by the jacket.

As for the waistcoat, it used to be backless, low-cut, and, whether single- or double-breasted, with no more than three rows of buttons. However, since men began to remove their jackets during the course of a long evening (something that never used to occur), evening waistcoats have acquired a full back and they close higher on the chest in the manner of their daytime equivalents.

In recent years cummerbunds have become increasingly popular. These items derive from military dress uniform in colonial India where they were worn as an alternative to the waistcoat. Made from the same material as the bow tie and jacket facings, a cummerbund is worn with its pleats facing upward. Of late there has been a trend for cummerbunds (and matching bow ties) to be in a variety of colors and patterns, but this has the disadvantage of spoiling evening dress's elegant formality and is unacceptable to the purist.

The same is true for the accompanying shirt which should always be white, of the finest cotton, and have a turn-down collar; wing collars are worn only with the dress coat. The shirt front can be pleated or plain and, if it does not have a fly-front placket, should fasten with a series of shirt studs—these ought to be made either of silver or, possibly, gold and feature mother-of-pearl, onyx, or some other semi-precious stone. In such circumstances, you should have matching cuff links to close your cuffs.

There has been a fondness to wear a regular black tie instead of a bow tie with a dinner jacket. Aside from suggesting you are an off-duty funeral director, this style also implies the inability to tie a bow

A plain black ribbed silk bow tie, matching the lapel facings of the jacket, will be worn at the neck. This should be self- and not pre-tied. There are two common styles of ties: the butterfly wing, which has a central bulge and flares at the end, and the bat wing, which has parallel sides. The second of these forms a smaller and neater bow, and is the preferable option. Beginning among actors and then emulated by their admirers, there has been a fondness to wear a regular black tie instead of a bow tie with a dinner jacket. Aside from suggesting you are an off-duty funeral director, this style also implies the inability to tie a bow. Neither implication does much for your credibility.

Socks will be black, of silk or fine merino wool, and knee-length, while shoes—also black—are either patent or highly polished Oxfords. The only acceptable accessories are a well-starched white linen handkerchief in the breast pocket and possibly a small flower as boutonniere.

Weddings

If you are attending a wedding, the invitation card may specify a dress code for the occasion. This is likely to fall into the following categories: a business (or lounge) suit; a dinner jacket; or morning dress.

The Business Suit and Dinner Jacket

The first of these requires you to wear a matching jacket and pants, together with shirt and tie. Fabric, color, and so forth will depend on the time of year, the weather, and your personal taste, although it is never a good idea to be better dressed than the groom (or the bride). The dinner jacket will be a black tuxedo and trousers with white shirt and black tie, as described on pages 94–97.

Morning Dress

Morning dress—which, despite its name, can be worn at any time during the day—is the most formal daytime dress code and is worn in Britain and Europe at formal weddings. The morning coat is a variation on the dress coat and derives from the same era, the late 18th/early 19th century, when a tailcoat cut for ease while riding became the norm.

The main element of morning dress is the morning coat, sometimes called a cutaway. It is single-breasted with the front meeting at one button in the middle, after which it curves gently away to conclude in a pair of knee-length tails at the rear, two ornamental buttons featuring here on the waist seam. In color it can be either black or Oxford gray and made of herringbone wool, with pointed lapels of the same fabric. The accompanying pants are usually in a thin gray and black stripe (very occasionally these are checked), with one or two pleats at the waistband; as with the dress coat, here, too, suspenders (braces) rather than a belt are worn to support the pants and ensure there is no gap between their top and the bottom of the waistcoat.

Traditionally the morning coat waistcoat was gray, black, or buff (a pale yellow-brown color), but of late it has become permissible to sport a waistcoat of any conceivable hue, especially at celebratory occasions like weddings. The same is also true of shirts and ties, although if you are not wearing a white shirt, it is best to opt for one that has a colored body teamed with white collar and cuffs. The shirt will have a turn-down collar. What remains firmly beyond the pale is the combination of wing-collared shirt and pre-tied ascot (or cravat) necktie beloved of dress-hire companies, especially when the ascot is teamed with a matching waistcoat.

Of late it has become permissible to sport a waistcoat of any conceivable hue, especially at celebratory occasions like weddings

Shoes will be black and plain Oxford, not patent, which is confined to evening wear, and not brogues. Your accessories are a white or patterned handkerchief in the breast pocket, a floral boutonniere, and, if you wish, gray or lemon gloves—preferably of suede or chamois—and a "white" top hat, which is actually gray in color.

Chapter 10

Casual and Sports Clothes

We live in an era of informality. Everyone addresses each other by first name on first introduction, for example, and sometimes even without it. The relaxed nature of our lives extends to clothing, in which formal style can play a minor role. But as the preceding chapters have indicated, there are occasions when we will be expected to dress in what is deemed the correct fashion and to conform to long-established formal rules. This may irk but unless you are a determined rebel—and frankly refusing to wear a jacket or tie is hardly going to mark you out as the fearless revolutionary of your generation—then it is simply easier to abide by accepted norms.

On the other hand, even in such bastions of tradition as the office, formality of dress is less prevalent. Think of the rise of dress-down Fridays, although that concept went into decline in the workplace after many people found it too hard to define an acceptable degree of casualness. What, after all, is the precise point at which relaxed dressing shades into sloppiness?

That question sums up the key issue with regard to all casual clothing: Just how casual can you afford to be? The phrase "smart casual" is certain to throw any recipient of an invitation bearing those dreaded words into a state of anxiety. Does it mean jeans and T-shirt? Or jacket and open-necked shirt? Or a point somewhere between the two? Most men find it hard enough to give how they dress any consideration without being required to negotiate the subtle nuances of "smart casual."

In fact, there is no need to do so if you adopt the principle that it is better to be too smart than too casual. Much of what you wear during the more structured part of your life will carry over without difficulty to casual occasions. The majority of your shirts, for example, will work in any circumstances, as will your knitwear and most of your shoes. Jackets can be dressed up or down according to circumstances; combined with jeans or chinos for a relaxed look, or teamed with something smarter as required.

The Golden Rules

Say you're asked to dinner and are unsure of the dress code. Wear a jacket and tie because you can remove either or both if nobody else is wearing them, but you can't put them on if you arrive in a sweater. Whenever you're unsure of a dress code, it's better to over- than under-dress. So here is the number one rule for informal dressing: You can always make yourself more casual but you can't make yourself smarter.

The second rule is this: Never confuse casual for scruffy. Jeans and sneakers should be clean, T-shirts unripped, sweaters without holes. Casual is not a euphemism for dirty, and even though your clothes are relaxed, a vigilant determination to look your best should remain.

The third rule is one you will know already: Examine your physique and wear only those clothes, colors, and styles that show you to best advantage. If you have thin arms and pale skin, for example, an orange and turquoise striped polo shirt is not going to do much for you. We can often see other people's errors of dress without recognizing our own, but the fundamental fact is this: No item of clothing suits us all and we should select from what is available accordingly.

You can always make yourself more casual but you can't make yourself smarter

One other point: A lot of casual clothing comes adorned with logos and other signs of the manufacturer responsible. If you wish to turn yourself into a walking billboard, that is your prerogative, but it seems incredible that you are thus willing to pay money in order to advertise someone else's goods. Fashion has always been full of illogicalities but this must be one of our own age's more extreme instances. Unless you particularly wish to promote the business in question, it is recommended you only buy clothing unembellished with logos.

That so many men who look well in a suit can suddenly appear absurd when dressed informally is indicative of the importance of giving due consideration to this area of your wardrobe. In other words, casual comes with a code; ignore it at your peril.

Pants

As mentioned before, if you have bought wisely most of your clothes will be sufficiently versatile to make the transition from smart to casual. You will, however, need at least a couple of pairs of pants, including jeans, that are strictly for informal occasions. Never try to wear suit pants without the accompanying jacket. Not only will they suffer from too much use but they always look like one half of a pair of twins cruelly separated from each other.

Chinos and Khakis

You will want to own at least one pair of chinos, which are either flat-fronted or pleated (the former looks better) and made from a cotton twill fabric. They first appeared in the United States after the Spanish-American War at the end of the 19th century, their name deriving from the word Chino, which is Spanish for Chinese. Though originally styled for the army, they quickly became popular among civilians and have remained so ever since, helped by the durable cloth from which they are made.

Khakis are made from a cotton or linen twill and lend your wardrobe a satisfactorily casual element

Khakis are similar to chinos and, like the latter, owe their origins to the British military, in this case the uniform of soldiers serving in India from which the word derives. Like chinos, khakis are made from a cotton or linen twill and they will provide your wardrobe with a satisfactorily casual element without allowing it to descend into the slapdash.

The same cannot unfortunately be said for cargo pants, which were initially intended to be worn by workmen when engaged in outdoor activities, and members of the American army. In order to allow free movement and to accommodate work tools and equipment, they tend to have ample accordion pleats around the waist and several patch pockets down the legs. Among the general populace cargo pants became popular as casual wear during the 1990s and were soon followed by a knee-length shorts version. But with their baggy shapelessness and especially when made in cheap fabric, it cannot be said that cargo pants do much to flatter the average male. Accordingly it is better not to allow them space in your wardrobe.

Shorts

Most of us look and feel our best when wearing the clothes to which we are accustomed. Hence the inherent problem with shorts: We don't don them very often and when we do it is rarely with any degree of flair. Shorts are essentially vacation wear and should be confined to the beach, the swimming pool, the deck of a boat. They ought not to be seen in an urban setting, unless by  urban we mean a small port in the Caribbean. Even in the coldest parts of North America and Europe, whenever the sun so much as hints at making an appearance some men feel an inclination to pull on shorts, and then step outside while wearing them. This is an action no sensible person should undertake, not least because it shows a want of consideration for our fellow citizens' feelings. Your legs, unfamiliar with daylight, will look less than alluring, their color and texture not dissimilar to uncooked dough. This look cannot be classified as either casual or sloppy: instead it must be deemed downright foolish. A man wearing shorts in the city deserves to be met with mockery.

How to Wear Shorts

On vacation, it is permissible to wear shorts if you choose a pair that shows you to best advantage and encourages the preservation of personal dignity. Bear in mind that flat-fronted styles are more slimming and that shorts to the knee look better on an older man (i.e. anyone over the age of 25) than those cut high on the thigh. Incidentally, there is no reason why your regular standards of cleanliness and tidiness should be lowered just because you are wearing shorts. They should be as immaculate as any other garment in your wardrobe.

As for accompanying footwear, loafers look better than any other shoes, sandals are permissible—provided they are not worn with socks—and sneakers just about tolerable, but do remember that the last of these have a tendency to grow fetid in hot weather, and so too will any feet encased in them.

Denim and Jeans

A gentleman should dress well but ought not to be a fogey. Therefore denim will have a place in your wardrobe and you will sometimes wear jeans. A hard-wearing cotton twill fabric, denim's name derives from Serge de Nîmes, the latter being the French city in which it originated hundreds of years ago. But its distinctive color appeared only after a German chemist, Adolf von Baeyer, invented a synthetic indigo dye and this was used to create the blue jeans that are now so familiar.

Origins of Denim

For a long time denim was worn only by workers. When Levi Strauss & Co was founded in 1850, it was as a supplier of overalls and other such clothing for miners and railroad builders, as well as cowboys and farmers. Only after James Dean was seen in jeans in the 1955 film *Rebel without a Cause* did the garment start being worn by large numbers of the young, for whom it was a symbol of rebelliousness against an older generation's conservatism. For this reason jeans and other denim garments were frequently banned from many smart restaurants and private clubs until relatively recently. It cannot be claimed there is anything radical about denim today; an example of global uniformity, it is worn by all ages and social classes, and crosses all boundaries of race and creed.

Wearing Denim

Three items of denim clothing are acceptable in your wardrobe: a pair of jeans, a shirt, and a short jacket. The jeans you wear must be as plain as possible, sitting on the waist (where they will be fastened by a belt) with rivet-reinforced pockets at front and rear and straight-cut legs. Boot-cut jeans flare down the length of the leg, but not to the extent that they can be considered bell-bottoms. They can look slimming and are often preferred by men carrying some extra weight around the midriff. As such they are a tolerable alternative to straight-cut jeans.

The durability of denim is a drawback for jeans manufacturers who are keen to introduce all sorts of changes, sometimes subtle, sometimes extreme, into the garments they produce so as to encourage further sales. Resist their blandishments and stick with the classic straight-cut style as this will prove most versatile and last longest. Steer clear of anything with low-slung waist or crotch, with pleats at the top or rips at the knee, extra pockets or loops, and varying patches of color. Buy jeans that are pure indigo blue, and understand that they will naturally fade over time and repeated washing. It is possible to buy denim jeans in other colors, but the only one you should consider is white, provided you are slim and prepared to put it through the wash after every wear.

Although denim has become synonymous with casual dress, it has the potential to look smart when teamed with other, more dressy pieces

The same policy applies to your denim shirt and jacket—the latter cut like a biker jacket so that it is cropped to sit on the hip and to fasten at the wrist. Both must be as plain as possible and carry no extra design details. You will then find that these items will prove themselves versatile and capable of being worn on almost any occasion. Although denim has become synonymous with casual dress, it has the potential to look smart when teamed with other, more dressy pieces. Don't be afraid to shake things up. A denim shirt, for example, can be worn with a suit or a jacket and tie to a formal event. Likewise your jeans if combined with a tweed jacket or a covert coat will look well in every situation. Never assume that because you are wearing something in denim, the rest of your attire must be equally casual. And never wear more than one piece of denim at a time. Instead, for maximum effect mix it with other styles and fabrics. Finally, do not think of wearing any items of denim clothing other than those already mentioned. The fabric may be adaptable to all circumstances but the same cannot be said of you clad in a pair of denim shorts.

Casual Jackets

The denim biker-style jacket—cropped and slightly darted to stop at the waist, collared, tab-fastening down the front and at the wrists—has already been mentioned. It is a variation of another staple in your casual wardrobe: the leather jacket. This is still worn by motorcyclists but has also been adopted by many men who have never been on a bike since they stopped pedaling to school. This is fastened by a zipper down the front, as popularized by Marlon Brando in 1953's *The Wild One* and thanks to him it has forever after carried a hint of menace never entirely dispelled, even when seen on someone pushing a cart down a supermarket aisle. As with similar items, choose the simplest style of leather jacket, unadorned by superfluous studs or tassels. Make sure it fits snugly on the shoulders and does not billow out on the body to create a "big girl's blouse" effect. And look for the softest, most supple leather you can afford as this will last better than cheaper options.

Other than shoes and gloves, the biker jacket is the only acceptable piece of leather clothing you should own. Avoid a leather coat, unless you wish to be mistaken for an extra in a vampire film. Likewise shun leather pants, leather waistcoats, and so forth: On the average male they look not so much intimidating as ludicrous.

Look for the softest, most supple leather you can afford as this will last better than cheaper options

Other casual jackets such as blousons and bomber jackets are more difficult to carry off with success. Keep away from anything with an elasticated waistband: Your stomach will have to sit either above or below it and neither option is going to present an attractive spectacle. What in the United States is called an Eisenhower or "Ike" jacket and in Europe a combat jacket—basically a variation of the biker style in wool or cotton—can look well provided you are not carrying excess weight around the midriff and have reasonably broad shoulders. The similarly styled windbreaker, which usually comes with a hood, is another item you might want to own.

While some of these jackets have been inspired by military dress, army surplus clothing is best left to moody teenagers. Camouflage prints were designed for blending into the desert or jungle landscape, not negotiating the shopping mall on a Saturday afternoon. If you must seek inspiration from army clothing, why not try to see the appeal of smart dress uniform? However, since that is unlikely to be the case, embrace civilian status and clothe yourself accordingly.

T-Shirts

You will own various T-shirts. Some of these—plain, white, and in the best available cotton—are to be worn under a shirt, especially with an open collar. Others are going to be in various colors but regardless of shade must always be cotton. Make sure your T fits, especially across the shoulders. In the same way that men frequently wear jackets a size too large, so they have a propensity to choose baggy T-shirts. These flatter nobody, so even if you have a slight paunch, opt for a T that fits—but does not stretch taut across the belly.

As already mentioned, if you wear a T-shirt bearing the maker's name and logo you will have paid money to become a walking advertisement and might just as well don a sandwich board. T-shirts with slogans are for people without a sense of humor; you should make your own jokes, not wear someone else's. Comic T-shirts cease to be funny faster than they relinquish their dye in the washing machine, and even the best jokes lose their worth through repetition.

Sports Clothing

At the outset sports clothing was designed to be worn only while engaging in exercise. Somehow certain items, most notably tracksuits, have become everyday dress for many people unlikely ever to engage in exertion more strenuous than a stroll to the local bar. You are not such a person and will therefore keep your sportswear for its intended place: the field and the gym. Tempting though it might be to don a tracksuit when buying the Sunday papers, resist temptation and dress properly. Never be caught in sportswear outside a sporting environment.

Points to Remember about Your Sports Clothes

✳ Keep them clean. When you take exercise, you are likely to sweat (you certainly ought to do so if the exercise is to have any point). Accordingly, wash after each wear must be your policy.

✳ While fibers have been developed for professional sports clothing, it is probably best to stick with natural materials, specifically cotton. These will allow your skin to breathe and stand up to repeated wear (and washing).

✳ For reasons already stated, try to avoid clothing festooned with the manufacturer's name.

✳ Sports clothing should be comfortable, so bear this in mind when making your purchases. Don't wear anything too snug since it risks becoming painful after a while. Furthermore, in places like a gym tight clothing can be a distraction for other people taking exercise.

✳ The last of these rules is especially relevant to swimwear. Skimpy briefs are strictly the preserve of competitive bodybuilders, and fitted trunks belong on Olympian swimmers. The rest of us should stick to shorts. With an elasticized or drawstring waistband, they should be cut loose on the leg. The precise length is your call, whether to the knee or somewhat higher, although not too much above mid-thigh is advisable. Hawaiian prints are popular among the young but are not to be recommended for the more mature. Stick to a single color or, if you want a pattern, go for a gingham or madras check.

Polo and Rugby Shirts

A couple of items of sportswear have broken the mold and made a successful transition to leisure wear, the polo and rugby shirts.

The Polo Shirt

The polo shirt actually originated on the tennis court. In 1926 René Lacoste, the French seven-time Grand Slam champion, designed for himself a white, short-sleeved, and loosely knit cotton piqué shirt with unstarched collar and buttoned placket, which he wore at the U.S. Open Championship instead of the traditional long-sleeved, button-up shirt. Following his retirement from tennis seven years later, Lacoste teamed up with a clothing manufacturer. Together they established the company which produced and mass-marketed what is now known as a polo shirt, because it was soon also adopted by players of that sport.

Since being featured in collections from American designer Ralph Lauren in the early 1970s, polo shirts have become a standard of men's casual dress and are an indispensable element of the modern male wardrobe. In design, they should scarcely differ from the shirt created by Lacoste, made of a loosely knit cotton piqué with a handful of buttons at the top of the main body and a soft collar capable of being turned up (the idea being that tennis players' necks could thus avoid becoming sunburned). They look best in soft, pastel shades and should fit well but not cling to the chest.

The Rugby Shirt

Now found as much off the field as on, rugby shirts are effectively a long-sleeved version of the polo shirt, albeit with a stiffer collar. The main body and sleeves of this item will often, but not always be banded in horizontal stripes of two or more colors, the collar remaining white and knitted cuffs encircling the wrist. While polo shirts can be teamed with a jacket and thus shade into that amorphous territory of "smart casual," rugby shirts are very definitely casual and cannot be dressed up. Keep them for weekend and vacation wear, especially during the winter when it may be too cold to get away with a polo shirt.

Sneakers

Sneakers, known as trainers in Britain, is the generic term for the sports shoes now worn by a large percentage of the population as its preferred daily footwear. In Britain before sneakers existed there were plimsolls, first developed by the Liverpool Rubber Company in the 1830s for beachwear. For much of the last century, plimsolls were synonymous with school gyms and compulsory exercise. This association, together with the rise of the sneaker, led to their decline, but they retain a certain nostalgic appeal and serve as alternative casual footwear to their near-ubiquitous rival.

From the late 19th century onward, the plimsoll's American equivalent was the sneaker worn by the general population when engaged in sporting activity: The famous Converse All Star basketball shoe was developed in 1917. Only in the 1950s did sneakers start to be worn off the court, especially by school-going teens. But it was the fitness craze of the 1970s, with its focus on jogging, that led to the explosion of interest in sneakers, not least because manufacturers concentrated on producing a shoe that would provide support for the entire body when running on hard surfaces such as street pavements. Since then sneakers have steadily grown in popularity, with new designs being produced annually and different brands competing with each other for a larger market share. It's likely most of today's sneaker devotees do not wear this footwear because of its athletic merits, but for reasons of comfort. Plus, of course, sneakers are easier to maintain than leather shoes.

Taking Care of Your Footwear

If you are going to wear sneakers do be aware of their limitations, not least the fact that although some men team them with suits, they are irredeemably an item of casual dress. They look fine with a pair of jeans, but, despite the best efforts of aficionados, simply appear out of sync with formal clothing, not least because of the essential heaviness of their construction and frequently elaborate design; contrary to what is sometimes proclaimed, sneakers are incapable of looking sleek and streamlined.

Another widespread disadvantage of sneakers—not an inherent fault but caused by neglect on the part of those wearing them—is that they quickly grow dirty and unkempt. The outcome is that they look more than ever unsuitable for smart dressing. Should you wear them, even at weekends, sneakers ought to be looked after and regularly cleaned. This will have the added benefit of prolonging their life, which is a blessing because popularity has had the effect of increasing their price.

Chapter 11

Grooming

Clothes are the packaging, you are the goods beneath. There is no rationale in taking trouble over the wrapping if what lies inside has been kept in poor condition. A car may appear to be in good repair, but its real mettle only becomes apparent once the engine is started. In other words, you should look after yourself and make an effort to be well groomed regardless of the amount of clothing you wear. It is worth taking trouble over your face, hair, and body daily; those few minutes will reap long-term benefits.

Facial Care

Men's skin is different from that of women, being some 20 percent thicker and firmer due to greater quantities of collagen and elastin which are both proteins. The downside is that male skin is also commonly coarser than its female equivalent, with larger pores and more active sebaceous glands leaving it prone to oiliness, blemishes, and clogged pores. There is also a greater inclination for men's skin to sweat.

For all these reasons, a regular skin regime is recommended, beginning with your face being thoroughly cleansed twice daily. Although your skin is tougher than that of women, it is still vulnerable to excessively aggressive cleansing. Choose a mild, soap-free cleanser (soap can strip skin of essential oils) and rinse using warm but not hot water until all of it is removed. Pat dry (don't rub) with a clean towel, preferably not the same one you use after emerging from the bath or shower, and make sure your skin is completely free of moisture.

Moisturizers, Creams, and Lotions

It is now accepted that men should moisturize their skin in order to maintain and even improve its condition. Every pharmacy and supermarket has a section dedicated to men's grooming in which you will find a number of inexpensive moisturizers, one of which will suit you. While the majority of men have oily skin, this is not always the case, and yours may be drier than most, so it is worth undertaking a little investigation to ascertain what moisturizer is right for you. Bear in mind that late nights, alcohol (which dehydrates the body), and nicotine will all dry out your skin, making moisturizing more necessary than ever. Drinking sufficient water will also help to keep you—and your skin—well hydrated.

The advantage of moisturizer is that regular daily use will help to keep your skin suppler and softer

You may wish to apply a separate cream to the area around your eyes, one specifically created for this purpose since that intended for the rest of your face is not as suitable. The advantage of moisturizer is that regular daily use will help to keep your skin suppler and softer than would otherwise be the case and, in addition, will go some way to reduce visible signs of aging. How much any one product can accomplish in this respect is open to question, but what cannot be disputed are the merits of wearing a moisturizer with a high sun protection factor (SPF)—at the very minimum factor 15 but preferably closer to 30. This should be applied daily and not just during sunny weather; you are at risk from skin damage and cancers such as melanoma throughout the year. Certainly you ought never to expose skin to the sun's rays without first applying ample protection, and then regularly reapplying it.

Because of their skin's enlarged pores and oiliness, many men suffer from blemishes such as blackheads and acne. These require particular treatments, which are now widely available in pharmacies or, in more severe cases, a consultation with your doctor, who will be able to prescribe creams and gels to improve the skin. There is nothing "dirty" about blemished skin—the majority of those with acne are zealous about cleansing—but our culture tends to find it unattractive. For this reason, addressing the problem will pay dividends.

Shaving

It has been estimated that during the course of a lifetime the average male will shave his face 20,000 times. Yet this is an activity where practice does not necessarily make perfect; precisely because it is such a mundane daily task, many men do not shave themselves well— and suffer as a consequence.

A Clean Shave

Follow these steps and the result will be a better, sharper shave than was previously the case.

Begin by softening your facial hairs. One way to achieve this is through wrapping the lower part of your face in a warm, damp face cloth or towel, as is often seen in old-fashioned barbers. Alternatively, only

shave after you have bathed or showered—the steam created during these activities will achieve the same effect.

Next, wet the area to be shaved and keep it wet while you apply a cream or gel designed to assist in the process. Use either your hand or, if you prefer, a shaving brush for this purpose. Shaving brushes date from a time when less sophisticated products were available and some assistance was needed to work up a good lather on the face. Today gels are often deemed preferable to creams because they help the blade glide over the skin and do not clog pores. Look for a product that contains glycerine as this lubricates and protects. Products containing alcohol, mint or menthol, or other fragrances should be avoided as these can sometimes cause a reaction to skin which is particularly vulnerable after being shaved.

Prepare your razor by allowing it to soak for a few seconds in hot water. There are as many different razors on the market as shaving creams/gels and you will have to investigate which one is best for you. Some of the newer models can be almost too aggressive and while we all want a close shave this should not be with the result that our skin is left feeling raw.

Shave by holding a specific area of skin taut with one hand while a razor held in the other glides across the surface and removes the hairs. Rinse the blade in clean water between each series of strokes as this will prevent clogging.

Begin with the sideburns and down one side of the face, then the other. Next tackle your neck, followed by your chin. Finish with the upper lip—hair is thickest here and needs longest to soften. Whether you shave with or against the direction in which your hairs grow is a matter of preference and practice; in some areas such as the neck, it is often best to shave with and then secondly against in order to ensure all hairs are caught. Try not to be too forceful in your approach or this could cause razor burn. If you cut yourself, staunch the bleeding and then apply a styptic pencil (available from pharmacies), ensuring no further blood flows nor infection occurs.

Once the entire area to be shaved is done, rinse your face with warm, not hot water. Follow with a further couple of rinses in as cold water as possible to close the pores.

Pat, but do not rub, the face dry with a clean towel. Allow a minute for the skin to settle and then apply an aftershave balm, most usually a lotion. This should be unperfumed (the chemicals can cause a reaction on freshly shaven skin) but may contain an antiseptic to assist in closing pores and prevent infection.

There are as many different razors on the market as shaving creams and you will have to investigate which one is best for you

Change your blade regularly, such as every week. Blades not only grow less sharp with age, but also become more susceptible to build-up of shaving cream/gel residue, which can cause skin infection. If you suffer from in-growing hairs—a condition familiar to anyone with curly hair—the best solution is to soak a face cloth in hot water and hold this over the afflicted area for a short period, then use a pair of sterilized tweezers to pluck out the hair causing the problem. Pat the skin dry and apply a little moisturizer.

Electric razors are preferred by some men but seemingly some 85 percent of the world's male population prefer a wet shave. On the other hand, you ought to own an electric razor: It is invaluable for tidying up any tufts of hair overlooked while wet-shaving or for running over the face on evenings when you have an engagement and want to look your best.

Washing

Although too much washing can lead to dry skin—the water stripping our bodies of their natural oils—we ought to bathe once a day. Whether you take a bath or shower is up to you, but it should be pointed out that baths use more water and are therefore more expensive. In addition to the face, it is important to cleanse daily the armpits and groin area, both of which hold large concentrations of the apocrine glands that become active during puberty. Wash these regions with a soap-free cleanser and rinse thoroughly, then dry yourself and apply a deodorant/antiperspirant.

All of us sweat after exercise, while overheated, and in moments of stress; when this happens we lose moisture from our bodies and leave certain salts like sodium and potassium on the skin surface. If not cleaned away, the build-up of sweat residue can result in body odor—BO—hence the importance of regular washing. Some men sweat much more than do others as a result of a condition called hyperhidrosis, the precise cause of which is unknown, although it can be treated with medication. For the rest of us, daily—or in hot weather twice-daily—bathing will ensure we remain fresh. The application of antiperspirant helps to keep us that way during subsequent hours of activity.

Cologne ought to work with your own natural aroma, not overwhelm it

If you wear cologne, the best time to apply it is immediately after bathing when your skin will be most receptive to absorbing the fragrance. Bear in mind that not everyone will respond to the cologne's perfume with as much enthusiasm as you; indeed a few people are allergic to artificial scent, so limit the amount you wear. Cologne ought to work with your natural aroma, not overwhelm it and everything else in the vicinity.

Oral Hygiene

One of your most engaging features ought to be your smile, but this won't be the case if you have poor teeth. It is possible, and sometimes necessary, to spend a lot of  money on dental work, with the result being a perfect set of upper and lower incisors. However, a basic daily care routine will help to minimize trips to the dentist, and keep down costs when you do so.

Brushing your teeth thoroughly twice a day is a basic prerequisite. This should take at least two minutes and cover back as well as front teeth. Start with the outer surfaces, working from the back forward. Try to spend some time on the inside of your teeth before finishing with attention paid to the biting surfaces. Always brush from gum to tooth and do not use a jerking vertical motion as this can lead to gum recession and the exposure of parts of your teeth not protected by enamel.

When finished brushing, you should floss, gently but firmly sliding a piece of floss up and down between each pair of teeth. Follow this with an interdental brush, a small device that will remove any bits of food that may have become trapped between teeth. Conclude with an antibacterial mouthwash, preferably one low in, or free of, alcohol.

Bear in mind that some food and drink is likely to discolor teeth. Villains include tea, coffee, and red wine; the more you consume of these, the more likely there is to be evidence of their intake on your teeth. Cigarette smoking is also harmful to your teeth—nicotine not only builds up stains but also inflicts damage on the enamel and gums.

You ought to visit your dentist regularly, say every six months, in order to have your teeth checked. If you have been taking good care of them the dentist will have little work to do but in any case your visit is a chance to have your teeth professionally cleaned so that they look their best.

Your Hair

Like your clothes, you should wear your hair in a style best suiting your features. It is worth taking a little trouble to find out what works for your facial shape and coloring, and then keeping to the same style. Not all men look well with very short hair, while few of us can carry off long hair, certainly after the age of thirty. There is usually a happy median which will be right for you.

Regardless of length you should have a haircut every month, even if this only entails the ends being trimmed. Otherwise the entire head of hair will show signs of neglect, especially at the back of the neck and over the ears. Ideally these areas should be tidied by a barber once a fortnight: a task that takes no more than five minutes but makes all the difference.

Hair Care

Just as important as tidiness is cleanliness. You must wash your hair but how often a week depends on a number of factors: how greasy it becomes over successive days, for example, and in what sort of environment you work and live. Another factor to be taken into account is the build-up of styling products in your hair which have to be cleaned out after a few days. Nevertheless, bear in mind that too much washing is harmful because it strips the scalp of naturally defensive oils and does not allow time for them to be replenished. Even if you wash your hair only twice a week, ensure you do so with a gentle shampoo and conditioner.

After washing and drying your hair, you will probably use products like a gel or mousse to style and keep it in place. Once more, do not overload your hair or this could cause an adverse reaction on your scalp. In addition, too much product is harder to remove when you wash your hair, so try to apply the minimum necessary.

No man likes going bald, but if this happens to you there is no point trying to deny or hide it. Once your hairline starts to recede, rather than engaging in elaborate drapery across the top of your skull that leaves you in permanent dread of a high wind, settle for a crew cut. This will look smarter and more honest than any other approach to incipient baldness, and also prepare you for the inevitable.

Dealing with Unwanted Hair

It is a strange but widespread phenomenon among men that as the hair on our heads disappears, more of the stuff materializes elsewhere, most notably sprouting from our ears and noses. Never an enticing spectacle, this is also both untidy-looking and terribly aging. You should trounce it at first sight, employing one of a number of electric trimmers on the market designed precisely for this purpose.

Similarly disproportionate quantities of hair that spring up elsewhere on the body can look unappealing and deserve to be removed, especially if you are planning to remove your clothing in public. While there's no need to go in for elaborate "manscaping," the elimination of heavy growth in areas such as your back and shoulders is to be strongly recommended.

Hands and Feet

Your hands do a lot of work but receive little thanks for their labors, and absolutely no attention on their maintenance. This is ill-advised because, like the rest of your body, a little time spent on upkeep will reap benefits. If you engage regularly or even occasionally in manual labor, it is worth protecting your hands both before and after such activity with the application of a cream made for this purpose. Rough, callused hands are not pleasant either to look at or to feel. They will let you down, particularly if you have taken trouble over the rest of your appearance. Buy a tube of hand cream and make a point of applying it every day.

Nail Care

Dirty, unkempt nails will reflect badly on you and cannot be tolerated. If you watch black and white films from the 1930s and '40s, you will frequently see the protagonist receiving a professional manicure. This procedure has now fallen out of favor among men, but it is perfectly possible for you to take care of your nails; an undemanding and simple procedure, it takes just a few minutes and can be done while you're sitting in front of the television. Begin by keeping the surface beneath your nails clean, using a brush designed for this purpose while you are taking a bath or shower. The shaped end of a nail file will allow you to remove any excess dirt. Gently nudge it between nail and skin without pushing too hard against the latter.

Using either scissors or clippers you should trim your nails at least once a week so that they are never more than about one-eighth of an inch (around 3mm) in length. Tidy the nail's edge by running an emery board along the top and leaving a smooth curve on each fingertip. Nail-biting is a childish habit for which there is no excuse in adulthood. Not only will it make you look puerile but your hands will look a mess, too.

Nail-biting is a childish habit for which there is no excuse in adulthood

Caring For Your Feet

Similar efforts should be made to take care of your feet, not least as a reward for the support they give you every day. A weekly foot-care regime will help to minimize odor and avoid the build-up of cracked, scaly skin and calluses. Take time one evening out of seven to soak your feet in warm water into which a little cider vinegar has been added. After a couple of minutes of soaking remove all areas of callusing—on the heel and around the top of your toes—with a pumice stone or exfoliating scrub, then cut and tidy up your toenails.

After drying your feet, apply a moisturizing cream similar to that used on your hands; this will minimize the build-up of calluses over the following week. And always remember that the quality of shoes you wear will have a direct effect on the state of your feet. Ill-fitting and poor-quality footwear should be avoided. If your feet are kept in good condition, you will be the principal beneficiary.

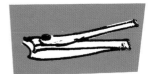

Index

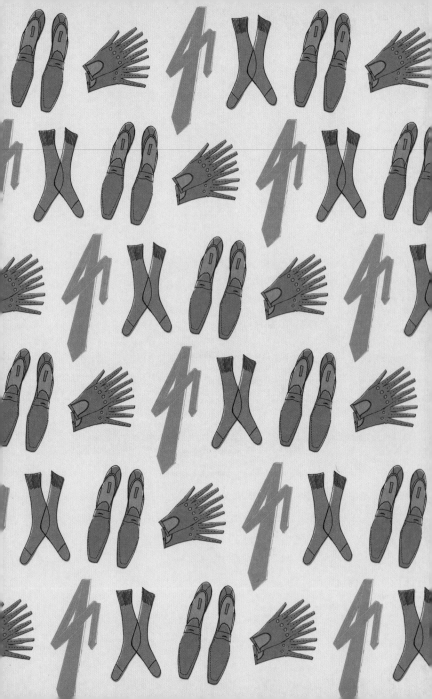